ABORTION

ABORTION

*A Mother's Plea
for Maternity
and the Unborn*

MARYBETH T. HAGAN

Liguori/Triumph
LIGUORI, MISSOURI

Imprimi Potest:
Richard Thibodeau, C.Ss.R.
Provincial, Denver Province
The Redemptorists

Published by Liguori/Triumph
An imprint of Liguori Publications
Liguori, Missouri
www.liguori.org

Library of Congress Cataloging-in-Publication Data

Hagan, Marybeth T.
    Abortion : a mother's plea for maternity and the unborn / Marybeth T. Hagan.—1st ed.
        p.   cm.
    Includes bibliographical references.
    ISBN 0-7648-1279-3
    1. Abortion. I. Title.

HQ767.H24 2005
363.46—dc22   2004061614

Printed in the United States of America
09 08 07 06 05   5 4 3 2 1
First edition

Contents

Introduction

For the better part of thirty years, I listened with ambivalence. I listened to the ongoing argument about abortion. During my freewheeling single days when secretarial jobs paid the rent, during a stint as an NFL cheerleader when I danced in the glitter of the often shallow world of glamour, during the rude awakening of a failed marriage, during a subsequent marriage blessed for twenty years, during pregnancies and miscarriages, during years as a stay-at-homemaker tending to infants, toddlers, the elementary school set, tweens and teens, and during my time as a midlife college student completing a bachelor's degree in journalism, I listened.

All along, my heart and my mind played tug of war over abortion. Maternal instincts suggested that the calculated end to a pregnancy, provided by abortion, might sooner or later leave a woman in a state of melancholy. I knew such a procedure would never solve anything for me. On the other hand, I was not everywoman. And who was I to determine how others should handle their pregnancies, especially those impregnated by power hungry sexual predators?

So, I kept listening. And the more I listened, the more I heard just one side of the story, particularly in the mainstream media. With the best of intentions, journalists sought to support equal rights for women. Too bad those good intentions grew distorted. Women's rights were reduced to one dimension as the media increasingly became a mouthpiece for the ever-enunciating voice of abortion advocacy.

Through my listening I developed a longing for a more humane message. God intervened and other messengers came. During pregnancies, the hearts that beat within me telegraphed sensations that offered clues to the wonders of the workings within the womb. One ultrasound, three special delivery babies, and several babies lost to miscarriage confirmed my gut feeling that the practice of abortion was barbaric.

Still, I listened.

During the completion of my bachelor's degree in midlife, professors at Temple University in Philadelphia helped me put feminism and abortion into historic perspectives. Other teachers, some of them professional journalists in Temple's School of Communications and Theater, guided me as I searched for my writer's voice.

Finally, I attended local pro-life fundraisers, special programs, and public protests—including the annual march in Washington, D.C., on the anniversary of *Roe v. Wade*. The people I encountered were predominantly peace-loving, often prayerful, anti-abortion activists; students, teachers, doctors, lawyers, construction workers, professors, Catholics, Protestants, Jews, atheists and so forth— indeed, a multicultural portrait of American society. Unfortunately, I discovered that the voice of this peaceful majority was consistently suppressed by the media in favor of the more rare, irrational, and often violent expression of a few anti-abortion activists.

Enough listening.

Our firstborn is a college student now. Her sister and brother are in high school. My husband and I still wonder how our children moved so quickly from the diaper derby to young adulthood. What choices will our children make when family planning becomes their reality?

It is time to speak. Since it has taken decades to clear my head and draw the conclusion that abortion is too wrong to be a right, please consider my musings on the issue. I have no desire to tell you what to think about abortion. No one could ever tell me what to think about anything. I only ask that you take some time to read the reflections of a person who never intended to become a pro-life apologist.

For the record, I also did not plan to become a pro-life writer. In my freelance commentaries, published in a number of newspapers over the past five years, I have covered a variety of topics. But like a demanding child, the issue of abortion insisted repeatedly that I give it my undivided attention. It nagged me. Only research and writing op-eds about abortion stilled the stirrings that interfered with the tranquillity of my soul.

My soul's search engine worked overtime and produced other results, sixteen chapters. I offer them to you in hopes that they stir something within, that you will contemplate the morality of abortion, and that the opinion you shape on the issue will be an informed one.

ABORTION

Chapter 1

Liberation From the
Romance of Reproduction

Not long ago, a child was described as a "twinkle," as in "I knew your parents when you were just a twinkle in your father's eye." That romantic notion died on January 22, 1973, when the U.S. Supreme Court ruled in *Roe v. Wade* that abortion was legal. Since then, we've lost more than 44 million twinkles.[1]

If the popular reality television series *Survivor* had been broadcast from the womb since *Roe v. Wade*, all the born of society would be the "survivors," and the aborted would be the "castaways," voted out of the reality of life.

As a baby boomer, I celebrated my twenty-first birthday just three months after abortion was legalized in 1973. I acquired several citizens' rights that year. I could finally stop breaking age-based prohibition laws and drink alcohol legally. I could finally vote. And if I happened to get pregnant, I could terminate that pregnancy with a medical procedure that would remove the embryo or fetus from my body.

While I toasted my newfound privileges and the 1920s suffragists who fought for passage of the U.S. Constitution's Nineteenth Amendment that granted women the right to vote, something about a woman's right to abortion left me feeling as if I had a hangover.

Women were skipping to a tune far different from the jump rope ditty that I sang with others as a child. "First comes love, then comes marriage, then comes Jane with a baby carriage" seemed downright fuddy-duddy as the women's movement advanced. The traditional sequence of events—love, marriage, family—fit the free love era like old-fashioned metal roller skates that clamped onto canvas sneakers with a key and flopped off repeatedly. Modern women put away those awkward skates, packed away worries about losing their key, slipped-on sleek Rollerblades, and raced full speed ahead into the fast lanes of the sexual revolution.

My friends who had abortions were unmarried. They were bright women who felt that their pregnancies were inconvenient, embarrassing, career threatening, or other. One friend's fiancé encouraged her to have an abortion during their engagement. She agreed, had the abortion, got married, and devoted herself to her career. Subsequently, while successful with her career, the abortion contributed to the failure of her marriage. Another friend had an abortion simply to maintain her glamorous single lifestyle. Both of them were law-abiding and hardworking. I doubt that either of them, and others like them, would have sought abortion as a solution if it had not been legal.

How did we American women come to this bend in our reproductive roads?

Serrin Foster, president of Feminists for Life of America, has traced the route and mapped every dangerous curve. According to Foster, The National Organization for Women included abortion in its list of demands in 1966 when it was founded as a special interest group to promote equal opportunity for women. Between

1968 and 1973, abortion advocates from another special interest group known until 2003 as the National Association for the Repeal of Abortion Laws, currently NARAL Pro-Choice America, convinced the women's movement that "it was fertility that was holding women back from equality in the workplace."[2] NARAL sold its fantasy about fertility to the public by first convincing the media "that the cause of permissive abortion was a liberal enlightened, sophisticated one," and in order to support this claim, "we simply fabricated the results of fictional polls."[3]

While there were nearly 100,000 illegal abortions performed annually before *Roe v. Wade*, NARAL regularly fed the media a heftier figure of 1,000,000. From 200 to 250 women died annually due to illegal abortions, but NARAL exaggerated that figure to 10,000 in order to paint a more vivid pro-life fantasy for the media.

Those who advocated abortion also focused on the necessity of legalized abortion for impregnated victims of rape and incest. In fact, the cold, hard figures reveal that few women become impregnated during rape.

Brian Clowes points to six major studies conducted during the past thirty years to make this case in his book, *The Facts of Life: An Authoritative Guide to Life and Family Issues*. Researchers examined the outcomes of 155,000 forcible rapes. The combined results of their studies revealed that "one out of 1,238 rapes results in pregnancy," which tallies to 0.08 percent or about one-twelfth of one percent.[4]

Human decency demands compassion for any woman, rape victims or not, who winds up in an emergency room or, worse, dead due to a botched abortion. Despite the sadness I felt for women who had experienced the horrors of rape, I could not reconcile my genuine sympathy for them with the heartlessness of abortion.

The disconnect between what I witnessed among friends and what I read in the media about abortion added to my ambivalence and left me sitting on the fence that divides Americans over the issue. My dismount was a slow one. My fuzziness about abortion took almost thirty years for me to shake.

Pregnancy and miscarriage taught me about the intangibles of reproduction, those illusive feelings of maternity that cannot easily be defined. Parenthood came late to me. I was in my thirties when the "twinkles" in my husband's eye morphed into the "glow" of my three full-term pregnancies. Another pregnancy lasted four months before ending in miscarriage the week before my fortieth birthday. Two more pregnancies ended in miscarriages during the first trimester.

Label me a hopeless romantic if you wish. But all my worldly experiences lacked luster compared to the sense of wonder I felt while pregnant or, as they used to say back in the day, when I was "with child." Each child I carried taught me something about life and death. Every pregnancy answered more of my questions about abortion.

Pregnancy, like a progressive dance, moves step by step through the creative process in the cloister of the uterus until the day of delivery. Like any work of art, newborns are the sum of all their developmental parts.

Each procreative dance of my pregnancies began with fluttery movements within my womb. Those first stirrings of evolving life occasionally brought with them nausea and often exhaustion. The rhythm of my babies' heartbeats, heard during first trimester maternity checkups, picked up the tempo.

A bigger belly made room for more movement by second trimester, and three of my offspring complied. The drama of their dances peaked as arm extensions and powerful kicks created bumps the size of acorns that protruded then disappeared from my midsection during the last few months of pregnancies. Finally, the doctor fished my tiny dancers from their amniotic fluid-filled worlds, and they were born into this one.

Chapter 2

Abort the Baby–
Adopt a Doll

While I was being introduced to the mysteries of bearing children just ten years after the U.S. Supreme Court ruled in *Roe v. Wade*, the country was introduced to the Cabbage Patch Kids. I wondered then, as I do now, what this 1980s fad for a to-die-for-adoptable-doll reflected about the subconscious sentiments of a nation where real developing babies were being weeded from the womb through legalized abortion.

Plenty of people owned and loved the cuddly dolls, as did my daughters. Xavier Roberts created his "Little People," first sold as soft sculptures at craft fairs, along with a unique marketing concept in the late 1970s. One-of-a-kind Little People came complete with names and birth certificates, and were available for purchase and "adoption." Roberts and his associates even renovated an old-time medical clinic in Georgia and converted it into Babyland General Hospital. Little People became legendary Cabbage Patch Kids in 1982 when Coleco was licensed to produce the dolls en masse.

Here's how "The Legend" of the Cabbage Patch Kids goes:

One day, a young boy named Xavier Roberts wandered into a magic cabbage patch hidden behind a beautiful waterfall. He discovered busy little Bunnybees sprinkling cabbages with magical crystals. Suddenly all sorts of different kids and babies peeked out of the cabbages! Each one had his or her own special look, personality, name and birthday. "I'll call you the Cabbage Patch Kids!" he said as everyone cheered.

Xavier fell in love with the "Kids" and built Babyland General Hospital just for them. It's a safe, happy place to live and play until someone like you takes them home to be cared for and loved.

When you adopt a "Kid"™ of your very own, you become part of the legend, too…and make a Cabbage Patch Kid very happy.[1]

Americans bought "The Legend" big time. Potential customers formed long lines outside of toy stores hours before scheduled openings in the early 1980s. When the doors opened, they pushed and shoved their way into the doll aisles, as if lives depended upon finding a Cabbage Patch Kid. Fad turned into frenzy. Fistfights followed when supply did not meet demand for the dolls. Police presence was required in toy stores. Some retailers instituted a lottery system to determine who would win the right to buy and "adopt" one of the Kids.

Meanwhile, women aborted the real deal. The Alan Guttmacher Institute records a total of 1,575,000 abortions in 1983 and another 1,577,200 in 1984.[2] Certainly, some of these aborted children in the United States might have had birthrights and been available for adoption if not for *Roe v. Wade.*

Once upon a time, most pregnant women who found themselves unable or unwilling to care for the occupants of their wombs discreetly delivered the babies and gave them up for adoption. Legalized abortion deleted an abundance of such deliveries in the United States. This greatly reduced the number of newborns in need of the gentle touch of adoptive loving care. (Even so, there are still plenty of orphans throughout the United States. Yet, more Americans adopt internationally, or invest in fertility treatments in hopes of pregnancy, regardless of the availability of homegrown babies in need of nests built with benevolence.)

U.S. babies with beating hearts in uteri were not afforded the same luxury as the manufactured Kids who lived in the "safe, happy place" known as "Babyland." NARAL created a fairy tale with a moral of its own: Fertility limits women from living happily ever after in the workplace. This myth effectively convinced many potential mothers that terminating a pregnancy would make all their wishes come true. These abortion advocates also introduced the term "pro-choice" in order to limit imagination about the gruesome details of the abortion procedure. NARAL's fractured fairy tale worked like a charm. While the group waved its magic wand over women in search of treasured equality, NARAL picked their reproductive pouches and robbed them of heredity by reducing a generation in the earliest stages of humanity to an object of choice.

Meanwhile, the society that defined a developing baby as a potentially disposable thing worked itself into hysterics over acquiring a doll. Now, there's a paradox for you!

By the end of 1983, more than 3 million Cabbage Patch Kids were "adopted." Coleco added a nursery line of Cabbage Patch "Preemies" and an animal line of "Koosas" in 1984. The company sold approximately 20 million dolls that year, and I delivered my first child.

Chapter 3

Babies Bearing Lessons

My daughter, Melanie, elevated our soon-to-be-parents' anxiety by refusing to leave her developing stage on schedule. Melanie's due date was July 11. She arrived four weeks later to welcome applause as Dr. Bruce Hopper lifted my firstborn high into the air. The relieved audience included her father and the medical personnel who assisted the doctor in performing my emergency cesarean section after a fetal monitor revealed that my baby was in distress. Anesthesia spared me from pain during the operation, but it did not numb the sensation of elation I felt over the safe arrival of my child.

In the first trimester of my next pregnancy, the doctor recommended ultrasound imagery to double-check the baby's due date. Ultrasound equipment produces a clear picture of life in the womb on a small screen through high frequency sound waves. After the technician moved the cool tip of the machine's magic wand across my stomach, I spotted contours of humanity on the screen. There I saw her round head, delicate profile, tiny limbs, and curled body attached to the cord that connected us. The technology even provided me with snapshots of my developing child.

The life I beheld through ultrasound opened my eyes and forever changed my views about abortion.

Random musings flash without warning in such emotionally charged moments. "That's my baby," I marveled to myself before the sledgehammer of a deeply disturbing introspection clobbered me. "How can we abort babies who look just like her every day?" my mind whispered. My heart ached and my soul shuddered.

Amy's fetal snapshot was taken toward the end of her first trimester. The ultrasound image is dated July 16, 1986. The newborn whose name means "beloved" arrived nearly six months later on January 12, 1987.

In 2002, news of legislation proposed in the U.S. House of Representatives sent me on a sentimental journey in search of that first picture of my middle child. When I found Amy's ultrasound photograph in an old jewelry box, I could clearly see why abortion-rights advocates were so worked up about the Informed Choice Act.

The bill (S.340) moved on to the Senate. It seeked to allow the secretary of Health and Human Services to offer grants to nonprofit health clinics for the purchase of ultrasound equipment. Clinics equipped with this common obstetrical technology could then provide women with unplanned pregnancies a glimpse of what is going on inside themselves.

Senator and Baseball Hall of Famer Jim Bunning (Republican) of Kentucky pitched the bill to the 108th Congress in February 2003. The bill was referred to the Senate Committee on Health, Education, Labor, and Pensions. S.340 will become a law if a majority of senators approve, more than half of the House agrees, and the president signs the bill.

When the Informed Choice Act was introduced in the House, Kate Michelman, the president of NARAL Pro-Choice America at the time, voiced her displeasure. She claimed that some crisis pregnancy centers, which do not provide abortion counseling, use ultrasound imaging to "intimidate" perplexed pregnant women: "It never fails to amaze me how little respect they have for women's capacity to understand what goes on in our bodies."[1]

At age thirty-four, I knew plenty about my body when I first spotted Amy in the pocket of my reproductive pouch. Ultrasound provided additional information. Surely, such knowledge enhances a woman's understanding of her body and educates, rather than intimidates.

If those who advocate "choice" were truly "pro-choice," wouldn't they want women to know as much as possible about their pregnancies, planned or unplanned?

The problem for abortion advocates is that ultrasounds breathe life into the "choice." The "choice" on the screen of the ultrasound machine sure looks like a "she" or "he." If it has fingers and toes like a baby and sucks its thumb like a baby, it is probably a baby.

Furthermore, since the "choice" appears to be a person, the decision to abort is a death sentence before birth. By bursting his or her amniotic fluid-filled bubble, abortion penalizes the innocent for being conceived in the wrong place at the wrong time.

Even though I never thought conception of an unexpected baby would happen to me, our last child to arrive intact was my first unplanned pregnancy. Melanie was three-years-old and Amy a six-month-old baby when I realized that the stork might deliver another bundle to diaper. Surprise!

Surprises can be good or bad things, depending upon the circumstances; most people enjoy the festivities at surprise parties, but very few would find cause for celebration if they were to become victims of a surprise attack. Those supporting abortion rights often apply the second approach and treat unplanned pregnancy as if it were an invasion. They view the result of that pregnancy as an antagonistic object that has attacked a woman's body, a foe that will rob her of freedom, an enemy she can oust with an abortion.

I chose to consider my unplanned pregnancy a surprise party and the baby I carried a gift from God. The doctor delivered my present on May 11, 1988. God gave me a son and my husband a similarly wired namesake. The French phrase *joie de vivre* means "joy of living." It describes someone who bursts with energy and love for life. As those who know the men in our household could tell you, *joie de vivre* characterizes Michael and Mike.

Chapter 4

Maternal Loss:
The Heart of the Matter

After sailing smoothly through three pregnancies, the progression of the next one hit me below the belt. Four months into the pregnancy, right before my fortieth birthday, the pregnancy terminated with a miscarriage. That's when I began to wonder about the emotional health of women who choose abortion and how they feel days, months, and years later.

The miscarriage required medical attention in order to cleanse my reproductive system. The piece of equipment necessary for the procedure whirred like a vacuum cleaner. The sound sickened me. My heart bled with my body.

Four months had given me too much time to daydream about a new family member. Would the child be a boy or a girl? What would be his or her uniqueness? Daydreams ended when a Power greater than me determined that he or she was not meant to be.

Two additional pregnancies ended even earlier in miscarriages. After the first loss, I never allowed myself the luxury of projecting tomorrows for the fetuses I carried. If I started to wonder about their features or futures, I stopped myself.

Since I accepted miscarriage as God's will and as nature's way of ending a pregnancy, I moved on with my life. Or so I thought. Once in a while, something triggered tears that accompanied the memory of my loss. One September day, five years after the first miscarriage, I sobbed as I drove past my children's elementary school. The child I lost would have been starting kindergarten that year.

After that tearburst, I began to wonder if women planning abortions ever daydreamed about the fetus within, or if they blocked such thoughts as I did after my first loss. I wondered what they thought about during the procedure as they drifted in and out of consciousness. I wondered if they ever speculated about the child who might have been. I wondered, but I never asked for fear it would be too hurtful.

Women who choose abortion suffer loss, too. If my hidden despair surfaced after an abrupt end to a pregnancy, surely other women experienced eruptions of sadness after abortions. My suspicions were confirmed. Today, a more compassionate approach toward women who opted for abortion has opened the floodgates to an increasing number of stories about emotional fallout after abortion.

Maternity comes with strings attached beyond the cords that connect mothers to their offspring. The occupant of a woman's uterus also touches her heart, unless her core was iced by life's cruelties, frosted after being coerced to abort, or chilled within a culprit possessed by self-absorption.

Every so often I watch the child who was my surprise pregnancy as he clowns around with his sisters, hustles in lacrosse or earns academic honors, and I wonder. I wonder if women who chose abortion feel the void of lost children in their lives. And I pray for a healing of their hearts.

Chapter 5

Not So Happily After Abortion

B efore I had even begun to suspect that some mothers suffered post-abortive heartache, Theresa Burke was already
working on a healing process for women who struggle with
intense "grief, not relief" after abortion. She has pursued this work
for more than twenty years.

In order to dispel politically correct myths perpetuated about
abortion within her profession, the psychotherapist created healing support groups and has written about her discoveries. I listened to Burke, along with an attentive audience at St. Norbert's
in Paoli, Pennsylvania, as she described her persistent efforts to
direct professional and media attention to those who suffer from
post-abortion trauma.

As a graduate student in the 1980s, Burke led a support group
for eight women who struggled with eating disorders. When one
participant spoke of post-abortion flashbacks and nightmares
about a baby, variations of agony erupted among five other
group members who had "buried the abortion chapters of their
lives."[1] The "avoidance" of dealing with the traumatic experience

of abortion, Burke concluded, is similar in effect to the symptoms of posttraumatic stress disorder.

Burke's meeting with the support group for eating disorders was only the beginning of her odyssey into the secret world of women who are faced with serious quality of life issues after abortion. The nationally certified psychologist would find this hush-hush universe to be heavily populated by women in need of consolation. Many who live there are shackled in guilt and shame, prisoners in solitary confinement with unresolved abortion-related grief. Family members and friends like me, who seal our lips to the subject of a loved one's abortion experience, only make matters worse.

Not only that, mental health professionals kept a lock on the treatment of post-abortion trauma. Burke told the group at St. Norbert's that the psychiatric medical community responded to her observations about post-abortive trauma with an unofficial we-don't-go-there doctrine. Those trained to unlock the intricacies of minds in misery labeled post-abortive problems "a private matter in sympathy with abortion rights" and did not treat the psychological effects of abortion.

Burke, who holds a doctorate of philosophy in counseling psychology, quickly learned that you cannot judge the aftereffects of abortion by its cover. Post-abortion trauma is not always evident shortly after the procedure because many women feel a sense of "it's over with" relief. Too often, memories and feelings about an abortion are kept neatly wrapped within. When those memories and feelings start to seep through years later, more than a few women who have aborted come apart at the seams.

The psychotherapist observed recurring symptoms of postabortive trauma during private and group therapy sessions with hundreds of women. Depression and self-destructive behavior due to unresolved grief also marked the stories of thousands of others who attended Rachel's Vineyard Ministries' weekend retreats and support groups.

Rachel's Vineyard is an international post-abortion healing ministry. Burke founded the ministry, which she codirects with her husband Kevin Burke. During retreats, a "living scripture technique" is applied to help participants of all faiths, as well as atheists, "face their anger, rage, grief, guilt, and inability to forgive themselves" after abortion.[2] Significant others are welcome to attend, because "the wound of abortion festers and pusses and infects so many other aspects of a woman's life."[3] Spouses, mates, mothers, fathers, grandparents, and siblings of the aborted offer mutual support, shared grief and sometimes seek their own healing.

This oozing of unresolved issues after abortion manifests itself in all sorts of unpredictable ways. Strange behaviors surface. Some of Burke's clients were already struggling with different problems before an unplanned pregnancy led them to abortion. Other women, whose lives were previously marked by stability, grew self-destructive after their abortions.

Like the women Burke first counseled in group therapy, some women starve, stuff, or purge themselves through eating disorders after abortions. Others prefer the numbing effects of alcohol or drugs. Some women become suicidal. Others experience abdominal cramping on the anniversary of their abortions. Quite a few women pine for another pregnancy hoping to find comfort in a "replacement baby." There are those who become obsessed with babies and those who simply cannot attend baby showers. Some women punish themselves by remaining in abusive relationships. Others sabotage healthy ones.

But what about women with terrible troubles that double when they become pregnant after being sexually abused or raped? How does post-abortion trauma affect them?

Being bound by a rapist, who camouflaged his face, invaded the privacy of her home, and violated her body in the summer of 2002, was harrowing enough for one Philadelphia woman. Months later the single mother of two little girls was stunned to learn that she was pregnant. She crossed the bridge into neighboring New Jersey and had an abortion in February 2003.

That was not the end of the rape victim's tribulations.

As if this woman had not suffered enough, genetic testing of the aborted fetus revealed that the rapist was not the baby's father. In January 2004, the victim testified in the trial that led to the conviction of serial rapist Alexander Drain. The *Philadelphia Daily News* reported on the trial in which the victim's testimony required making public the most personal aspects of her private life and reliving the attack once more:

> As she described the circumstances leading to the abortion—including her confusion of her menstrual cycle dates, the rape, her sexual relations with her boyfriend, and the fact that she had been given the morning-after pill hours after the attack—the woman began to cry. Her voice quaked as she told prosecutor Jason Bologna she was opposed to abortion but felt she had no choice.[4]

Victims of rape who choose abortion become victims of post-abortion trauma and public exposure, too.

For as long as I can remember, abortion advocates have soft sold abortion as the only compassionate response to the unplanned pregnancies of women victimized by the perverted who seek power through forced sex. However, there is more to the story.

The 194 testimonies in *Victims and Victors, Speaking Out About Their Pregnancies, Abortions, and Children Resulting from Sexual Assault,* edited by David C. Reardon, Julie Makimaa, and Amy

Sobie, reveal that abortion sometimes leaves women who become pregnant after rape torn apart by conflicting feelings.[5]

David Reardon, director of the Elliot Institute, is a biomedical ethicist, author, educator, and longtime researcher specializing in the study of abortion's aftereffects. According to Reardon, many victims of sexual assault "report that their abortions felt like a degrading form of 'medical rape.'" Reardon explains:

> After any abortion, it is common for women to experience guilt, depression, feelings of being "dirty," resentment of men, and lowered self-esteem. These feelings are identical to what women typically feel after rape. Abortion, then, only adds to and accentuates the traumatic feelings associated with sexual assault. Rather than easing the psychological burdens of the sexual assault victim, abortion adds to them.[6]

Understandably, women who have abortions after being raped make such associations; in rape cases, sexual assailants—usually masked or often strangers—inflict pain and leave women to their own devices for what might or might not be recovery.

The issues facing women who have been impregnated by sexual predators are also addressed by Dr. Theresa Burke:

> The experience of abortion as a violation of a woman's physical integrity is likely to be even more pronounced in women with a history of being sexually abused or raped. In these instances, the abortion is a connector to these other traumas. This is why a history of sexual abuse is a risk factor for greater post-abortion psychiatric problems. Adding trauma on top of trauma is not healthy, even if the victim is freely consenting to the abortion.[7]

Why is abortion such a stressor, a stress that for some women can be traumatic?

Clearly, as Burke points out, "Abortion touches on three central issues of a woman's self-concept: her sexuality, her morality, and her maternal identity. It also involves the loss of a child, or at least the loss of an opportunity to have a child. Women lose an element of their essence when they choose abortion. Naturally, the loss of this inherent and transcendent quality causes pain, not gain."

Chapter 6

One Life Lived in Post-Abortive Pain

Jeanne Stagloff never planned on the perennial aches she experienced after an abortion on April 19, 1985. Not the discomfort of cramping or heavy bleeding during the following week, but the emotional stuff that lasted eighteen years.

"No one ever talked about the pain," Stagloff recalls. No one at work. No one at the abortion clinic. No one who served as her support system after her abortion. No one, year after year after year, because her abortion had been a "real secret."[1]

Stagloff was living a liberated woman's dream come true when she realized she was pregnant. She had just completed her master's degree and landed a great job. When lunchtimes found her craving and devouring egg salad, a dish she could never before stomach, Stagloff just knew. A home pregnancy test confirmed the thirty-five-year-old single woman's suspicions.

After Stagloff lost it in the office one day, she told her new business associate about the unplanned pregnancy. He claimed "that he did not want to tell me what to do." Her managing partner made innuendoes about how babies stifle careers and provided her with an abortion doctor's name and telephone number that he just happened to have handy.

Stagloff called the recommended doctor and an abortion clinic in Philadelphia. She remembers sitting with her new title at her new desk in her new office, telephone in hand, telling the woman on the phone at the abortion clinic about her dilemma. Although Stagloff cannot recall the name of the clinic, she will never forget the woman's one-sentence response to her inquiry: "Well, you could either have *it* or you don't have to."

One detail addressed with clarity at the clinic was the price range. Stagloff recalls three different fees for "three different degrees" of consciousness available during an abortion and something about the word "twilight." (One Philadelphia abortion clinic in Center City offers: local anesthesia, which numbs the cervical area while the mother remains awake; general anesthesia, which puts a mother to sleep; and "twilight" anesthesia, which sedates the mother intravenously during an abortion.) In other words, more money bought a mother more unconsciousness.

The businesswoman experienced a Twilight Zone moment after climbing the stairs that led to the clinic: "When they could not even find a Band-Aide in the clinic for me because somebody misplaced them, I said to myself, '*These* people are going to perform my abortion?'"

The prior-to-talk about abortion that Stagloff anticipated from someone at the clinic never transpired. She chastises herself for not asking more questions before aborting forty-seven days into her pregnancy. "It never entered my mind to be educated about it," she admits. "People research all sorts of things," she wonders, "why not abortion?"

Stagloff spent the evening after her abortion at home in the company of a female friend and the man who fathered her aborted baby. Even though they both knew about Stagloff's abortion, the conversation centered on their children playing soft-ball.

Two weeks after the abortion, Stagloff was "shocked" out of her ignorance about the world in the womb while watching a PBS program about fetal development.

Five months after her abortion, Stagloff was fired from her job. Despite later career highlights, her confidence diminished. She continued to drink heavy doses of alcohol for several years thereafter. The sight of egg salad nauseated her. Like the women in Theresa Burke's support group, she had eating disorders. She struggled with anxiety.

Stagloff lost count of all the self-help books she read over the years. Even her decision to stop drinking fifteen years ago did not diminish her woe. During nearly two decades in and out of therapy, this woman never talked about her abortion. "You're just supposed to suck it up and move on," she grumbles as she thinks back. "Just do it on your lunch hour! That's the way it felt at the abortion clinic."

Meanwhile, she regularly struggled for an appropriate response when new acquaintances in business or social settings asked, "Do you have any children?" An answer of "no" left Stagloff wonder-ing if she was telling a lie. Parents who lose children to natural deaths can talk about it openly. "Society's stigma" dictates that mothers who abort must keep it to themselves, along with any regrets they might harbor.

Eighteen years after her abortion, Stagloff found a place where she could talk about it. "God's whispers" guided her to attend a Rachel's Vineyard post-abortion weekend retreat in March 2003. For Stagloff, and many other women, healing begins with being able to talk openly about the experience. She insisted that I use her real name in telling her story.

The "nurturing" and nonjudgmental atmosphere she found

at Rachel's Vineyard helped Stagloff to pinpoint the "core" of her pain. She dug up her deep regrets and grieved the loss of her never-properly-buried baby, realizing that she was a mother, a mother of sorrows. As a single, fifty-three-year-old woman without children, Stagloff muses:

> You don't know what's ahead of you. I keep wondering, if it were presented to me differently, what I would have done? There are so many unknowns with abortion. There's no chance to change your mind [afterwards]. At least [with adoption] there's some hope for your child.

Instead of hope, mothers who abort are left with dreams of their unborn children, dreams that cannot come true. During conversations with others whose pregnancies ended in abortion, Stagloff learned that her daydreams about what sex her baby might have been were not unique. Stagloff supposes that with some sort of "support" when she was pregnant, she might never have attended a Rachel's Vineyard post-abortion healing retreat.

Instead, Stagloff says matter-of-factly that she might have joined others in celebrating the accomplishments of the high school Class of 2003. "My child would have been graduating from high school this year," she remembered on the day I interviewed her. "It might not have been perfect. He might have had some problems, drugs, or something, but…." There would have been hope.

Rachel's Vineyard offers participants the opportunity to name their aborted children, if they wish, and honor them in a memorial service. Stagloff named her baby, whose due date was December 3, 1985, Luke Jacob. She has found a ray of hope in her belief that "I know where he is and my mom is with him."

Stagloff borrowed a sentiment from Margery Williams' *The*

Velveteen Rabbit, a popular children's book first published in 1922, and included it in a letter she wrote to her son. Stagloff searched for tissues as she told me about the letter. Her voice was a whisper. She had difficulty holding back the tears: "I told Luke Jacob, I told my baby, I loved him enough to make him real."

One of Williams' characters in *The Velveteen Rabbit* defines "real" for the Rabbit. "Real isn't how you are made," said the Skin Horse. "It's a thing that happens to you. When a child loves you for a long, long time, not just to play with, but REALLY loves you, then you become Real."[2]

What remains real, as well, for Stagloff is the pain: "I don't want to tell anyone whether to have an abortion, I just want women with unplanned pregnancies to know about the pain." She wishes that women considering abortion could participate in an "abortion education weekend" before making their decisions, a program like the pre-Cana classes that couples preparing for marriage in the Catholic Church attend to introduce them to the realities of that life-altering decision.

Jeanne Stagloff takes full responsibility for her actions back in 1985. Still, her story is one of betrayal. And it was not just the men in her life who let her down. Women who promised that abortion would be the key to Stagloff's and everywoman's liberation did, too.

Who is kidding whom? Abortion emancipates men far more than it does women. This ugly end to pregnancy frees selfish males from responsibility for their sexual activities. While some men experience sadness or guilt about a partner's abortion, it's women who endure the bloody procedure and, as time has finally told, women who suffer horrendous aftereffects.

America's callous if-you-get-pregnant-you-can-get-rid-of-IT attitude hurts us all.

"We are NOT disposable" read the large print on a bumper

sticker I spotted during a jog through my neighborhood. Must be a pro-life slogan new to me, I supposed? The smaller print was a blur, so I stopped for a closer look at the parked car and tried to make sense of the words, "If you don't...don't breed" on the sticker. Nose to the rear bumper, I finally managed to see the phrase, "If you don't rescue, don't breed."

The illustration of a trash basket full of adorable puppies made the intent of the tailgate proclamation clear. This was a noble effort to encourage breeders of dogs to be responsible and take back puppies if their home-sweet-home situation after leaving the litter turns sour. It was sponsored by Rottweiler Bros. Farm, a firm that markets merchandise for dog lovers.

Save the puppies. Protect the whales, the dolphins, and the wood stork.

Abort unwanted babies. Welcome wanted ones. Accept a legal procedure to end pregnancy that pollutes mother's nature, but when you have a baby be sure to deliver naturally. Better breast-feed, too. Welcome to the land of mixed messages.

Messengers of abortion advocacy send signals that often seem scrambled. Yet, their methods have been effective in convincing Americans, including me before motherhood, that the aberration of sacrificing our human unborn is socially acceptable.

Chapter 7

You Can't Judge a Cause by Its Cover

Words played a powerful role in advancing and maintaining the idea that the quick fix of abortion would balance sexual inequality. Pioneers of abortion advocacy mass marketed a word that has effectively contributed to social acceptance of abortion. NARAL wins the prize for the most creative use of a word to corral public support for abortion by framing it as "choice."

This artificial sweetener of a barbaric procedure has replaced the word *abortion* for many in the land of the free and the home of the overly caffeinated. Choice in reference to abortion has wiggled its way into our vocabulary because a society racing to keep up with responsibilities rarely has time to sip slowly and ponder the implications of jargon that suggest speedy solutions to complex problems.

Abortion advocates' manufactured meaning for the word *choice* proved to be such a powerful public relations tool that NARAL included it in its latest name change.

Just like fashionistas who stay on top of trends and dress

accordingly, NARAL changes its name to suit the times. The group began as the National Association for the Repeal of Abortion Laws. Its image makeovers after *Roe v. Wade* include the National Abortion Rights Action League, then the National Abortion and Reproductive Rights Action League and now NARAL Pro-Choice America.

NARAL's two earliest identities accurately described the group's purpose: to promote abortion rights. The word *reproductive*, added in the third rendition, is oxymoronic; any linkage of abortion to reproduction is ridiculous. There is no reproduction when a woman has an abortion.

As for rights that might qualify as reproductive, how about the right of a woman with an unplanned pregnancy to see the embryo or fetus she carries on federally funded ultrasound equipment before making a decision to abort? The Informed Consent Act or S.340 seeks to fund this right as mentioned earlier. NARAL staunchly opposes it.

Maybe that is why the now-you-see-it, now-you-don't phrase "reproductive rights" has disappeared from NARAL's new name, NARAL Pro-Choice America. This moniker also keeps the word *abortion* up its sleeve. Rather than *abortion*, what you see is *choice*, the winning card that NARAL has long flashed to gloss over an abortion's harsh realities both during and in its aftermath.

NARAL applies phrases like *reproductive rights* and words like *choice* to obscure the fact that every aborted embryo or fetus was a developing human being.

The abortion advocacy group added the word *America* to its logo after the tragic September 11, 2001, terrorist attacks brought red, white, and blue back into style. Forget Ralph Lauren's fashionable flag wear and Tommy Hilfiger's nifty logo. The NARAL Pro-Choice America label suggests that abortion is somehow patriotic.

NARAL's favorite accessory, Planned Parenthood, made a more perverse fashion statement about abortion following the blasts that toppled the Twin Towers and gave rise to a national river of tears. Planned Parenthood of New York City offered free abortions there from September 18 through 22, even as shocked family members and friends posted pictures of loved ones missing in the World Trade Center rubble and we, as a nation, pondered the fragility of life.

If the more than 44 million potential U.S. citizens denied birthrights due to legal abortion could speak, I doubt they would stand up and cheer for NARAL or Planned Parenthood. Many of their heartbroken mothers, veterans of post-abortion grief, guilt, and depression, might also tell you that abortion is overrated and simply not worth the price.

Abortion advocates aggressively prescribed abortion as the cure for inequality in the early days of the women's rights movement. (Even now they offer little or no fine print revealing the negative side effects of abortion's quick fix.) This boisterous push for reproductive rights dominated the women's movement for equality during the late 1960s and early 1970s. It also convinced masses of women that sacrificing the depersonalized unborn for self-fulfillment was the only way to be a bona fide feminist.

Those were the days when my friends and I from Philadelphia's Germantown neighborhood joined pals from Kensington's red brick row houses in slurping suds at parties known as "Beef and Beers." I always gave Mole time to catch his breath after performing his rousing Mick Jagger routine. With chin thrust forward and fist punching the air, the rhythmic round man shimmied effortlessly across the vinyl floor singing one of his favorite hits from the Rolling Stones.

As the title suggests, "Under My Thumb" tells of the thrill of domination that the crooner experiences in gaining control over his girlfriend's actions—how she dresses when she is permitted to speak, and even who she is allowed to look at. She's kept like a pet, with fewer rights than a "squirming dog" or "Siamese cat."

So, when the music ended and Mole plopped into a metal folding chair, our regular debate about women's rights began. Its recurring theme was equal pay for equal work. Since I was putting myself through my first two years of college, money was on my mind.

While I was just trying to make ends meet in the early 1970s, a book first published in 1963 was changing women's history. Betty Friedan's *The Feminine Mystique*, an examination of the stifling culture that pressed women into the starched roles of wife and mother, and Friedan's Ivy League perspective meant little to me at the time.[1] As they used to say back in those days, I could not "relate."

The "our mothers" described by Friedan in her book were loved, often highly educated, but not chosen as role models by their daughters. And they did not resemble my mother. "Did we understand, or only resent, the sadness, the emptiness, that made them [our mothers] hold too fast to us, try to live our lives, run our fathers' lives, spend their days shopping or yearning for things that never seemed to satisfy them, no matter how much money they cost?" Friedan asked.[2]

Unlike the mothers in Friedan's sphere, when my faith-based, high-school educated, literature-loving-homemaker mother headed toward local department stores, it was usually to buy my three growing brothers or me new clothes. Our charming, storytelling, truck driving, overtime-working father shopped for groceries on payday. And when an expired appliance needed replacement, the trip to Sears and Roebuck was a family affair.

Friedan's insights into the nameless void that homemaking can create for some women made more sense to me later in life.

After graduating from high school in 1970, I spent fifteen years as a wage earner in either Philadelphia's urban or New Jersey's seaside workforce. As a result, staying at home in suburbia with my first baby in the mid-1980s made me feel like a foreigner who needed a crash course in new language while already living in a strange land. Martha Stewart was never my hero and attempts at PTO involvement failed to fire my passions. Some days as a housewife were frustrating. Still I would not trade those unrushed times of intimacy with my little ones for anything.

Granted, I did not have the dilemma of putting a fabulous career on hold in order to stay at home with the children, as some women today do. But I did feel the sting of certain women's disapproval of my homemaker status when an end-of-conversation silence ensued after I answered their question, "What do you do?"

Ironically, housewives like me were considered a caste of knownothing cookie-makers by some feminists in the work world during the 1980s and 1990s, in much the same way that the stay-at-home casserole and cake-bakers, described in *The Feminine Mystique*, categorized career women as freaks of mother's nature decades earlier.

Still, I am grateful to Friedan and other feminists for seeking and finding better ways of life for women. Without their efforts, I might have been pigeonholed into homemaking. Instead, I chose it. My gratitude also extends to the author and other pioneers in the National Organization for Women, who revived the battle for passage of the Equal Rights Amendment in 1972, even though their efforts failed.

"Equality of rights under the law shall not be denied or abridged by the United States or by any state on account of sex," read the ERA to the U.S. Constitution that was first introduced in 1923 by suffragist Alice Paul, a militant who regularly picketed President Woodrow Wilson's White House. Congress passed the

ERA in 1972 and sent it to the states for ratification. The original juridical process required thirty-eight states to accept the amendment within seven years. In 1977, five years after its delivery from Congress, Indiana became the thirty-fifth and last state to ratify the proposal, leaving it just three states shy of becoming a constitutional amendment. Ironically, this last vote in favor of the amendment was cast in the same year as the death of Alice Paul. Congress ended up extending the seven-year deadline to 1982, but no new states were acquired. The ERA was reintroduced into Congress in 1982 and has been proposed before every session of Congress since that time. Unfortunately, it has never again been sent through the ratification process.

Had the ERA passed shortly after its acceptance by Congress in 1972, perhaps the connection between the rights of women and abortion would have been lessened or eliminated. One might also imagine the diminished impact of *Roe v. Wade* in 1973 and, furthermore, the safety of the otherwise aborted lives during subsequent generations. So, too, the principles of Alice Paul—who herself opposed abortion as the "ultimate exploitation of women"[3] —could have been vindicated solely on the basis of equal rights instead of as a platform for the propagation of abortion.

The ERA defeat added muscle to feminist efforts to strongarm the women's movement into adopting philosophies advocated by another mother of feminism, Margaret Sanger. Sanger founded the American Birth Control League in 1921, an organization that has been known as the Planned Parenthood Federation since 1942.

During her career as a nurse in the slums of the Lower East Side in New York City, Sanger was appalled by immigrant women's ignorance about their bodies, high rates of venereal disease, and especially by the death of Sadie Sachs. Sachs died due to a failed attempt at self-abortion in 1912. Sanger often told the Sadie Sachs

story to make her point about the need for contraception information.

By 1920, an upper-class concern over the declining white,
native, Anglo-Saxon birth rate grew alongside an anxiety about
overbreeding among immigrants. Sanger's commitment to her
cause appears to have exceeded her compassion for immigrants like Sadie Sachs. While Sanger still advocated birth
control for the poor, she pitched birth control to the rest of society as a way to protect them from the "prolific alien poor and
'unfit.'"[4]

For Sanger, birth control—specifically in the form of contraceptives—was a way to safeguard a society that was already growing too quickly.

Unfortunately, some feminists, who upheld the principles of
Margaret Sanger and the Planned Parenthood Federation, advocated abortion as a viable alternative for contraceptives. Such feminists who followed in Sanger's footsteps succeeded in creating
the illusion that if one was not for abortion, one was also not for
the liberation of women. Essentially, the philosophical principles
of Sanger, like Alice Paul, were wrongly associated with abortion.
Because the targets of Sanger's relief program, yesterday and today, tend to be minorities, anti-abortionists can conclude that
such feminists who advocate abortion as a sort of ethnic birth
control are thereby endorsing genocide.

While most of the United States' never-to-be-known aborted
posterity has been white, the largest percentage per capita of persons lost to abortion comes from minority groups.

Brian Clowes, director of Human Life International, presents
evidence in *The Facts of Life* that a disproportionate number of
minorities have ended pregnancies through "surgical abortion."[5]
More than 27 million white women and 14 million minority
women have had abortions since its legalization. "Because about

49 million minority people currently live in the United States," Clowes explains, "this means more than one-fifth of the country's minority population has been wiped out by surgical abortion."[6]

From 1980 through 2000, white women accounted for 65 percent, or 986,000, of annual abortions while minorities accounted for about 35 percent, or 531,000, abortions per year. During this same time period, 25.2 percent of white women's pregnancies were aborted, compared to 40.7 percent of minority abortions. Clowes concludes: "This means a pregnant minority woman is 62 percent more likely to abort her baby than a pregnant white woman."[7]

Care Net, which operates a nonprofit network of 700 pregnancy resource centers in the United States and Canada, offers statistics about "Abortion in Black America" that should horrify feminists of all persuasions. The group refers to abortion as "a silent killer in our community," a killer that takes the lives of 1,200 black babies every day.[8]

Care Net reports that "African American women abort at a rate of 529 per 1,000 live births"; whereas, the rate of abortion for white women is 177 per 1,000 live births.[9] Clearly, when one out of every three pregnancies in the black community ends in abortion, the loss is tragic.

Clowes also notes that "high minority cities have more than *three times* the number of abortionists per million citizens than low minority-cities."[10] He concludes, "Obviously, in this case, the huge surplus of abortionists in minority areas is the primary factor causing a large disparity in abortion rates between minority and White women."[11]

Not only that, Clowes points to a disparity in death rates among white and minority women who abort. Minorities suffer the greatest losses in mothers' lives due to "grossly substandard 'care' to them during abortions."[12]

"So-called 'safe and legal' abortion" was responsible for the deaths of 245 women, according to a study conducted by Human Life International. Clowes points out that of the 245 deceased, the races of 166 women were "positively identified" as "81 Blacks, 29 Latinas, 4 Asians, 1 Native American, and 51 Whites," which "means that 69 percent of the identifiable legal abortion deaths have occurred among minority women."[13]

The mythical magic bullet of legal abortion that is silently killing a disproportionate number of minorities in America has backfired in other ways, too.

For as long as I can remember, advocates have sold abortion as a woman's required ammunition to fight for her rights and advance in all areas of her life. But it was the 1972 passage of Title IX that granted women equality in educational programs and extracurricular activities. Title IX, not the *Roe* decision, opened doors to more opportunities than ever before in academics and athletics for women. And it was good old-fashioned hard work and determination that helped women to make the arduous climb into the upper stratosphere of the workforce where many belong, not *Roe*.

Today abortion advocates tell us we have much to fear. They claim that if we lose rights granted by *Roe v. Wade*, all of women's societal gains will go. Fear not. It simply is not so. There is nothing magical about *Roe* that necessarily leads to the betterment of women's social position.

"Women at Work," a study released by the American Association of University Women (AAUW) in 2003, finds more women in the workforce and more in managerial or professional occupations today, but most women are "still largely pigeonholed in 'pink collar' jobs."[14] The most common occupations for women are secretaries, bookkeepers, sales supervisors, nurses, waitresses, receptionists, and cooks. The highest proportion of college-educated women in the workforce maintain careers in teaching or nursing just as they did back in the 1960s. "Women at Work" highlights the need for a greater concentration on advanced science, engineering, and computer technology in women's education as a way to close the high-tech gender gap.

Another troubling gap exists that divides women. That is, more females than ever graduate from college alongside a near equal number of males; but unfortunately gains in educational opportunities apply only to certain women. As the AAUW report states:

> Educational progress, for example, continues to vary by income level and by race-ethnicity. Latinas, a disproportionately low-income population, lag markedly behind as the only group that averages less than a high school education. The women most likely to be employed in fast-growing fields with higher-than-average wages are Asian American (8.9 percent) and white (8.7 percent). Native American women are the least likely (4 percent) followed by African American women (5.7 percent) and Latinas (5.8 percent).[15]

Abortion was supposed to deliver all females to the promised land of equality. What happened? How did we come to believe that removing the fruits of the womb would balance the scales of justice for anyone? Let's keep counting the delusive ways.

Chapter 8

Abortion Advocates Give Birth to the Pro-Life Stereotype

W hen abortion advocates stole the women's rights show, they also mastered the art of enchanting the media. In sincere efforts to support gender equality, the media allowed itself to be seduced by activists that warned about the essentiality of abortion to advance women's rights.

Meanwhile, there was another voice: the unassuming voice of the typical abortion protester—a wallflower to the media—who rarely qualified for an invitation to speak to the public. She still hummed lullabies as abortion advocates around her belted out "I Am Woman, Hear Me Roar." Her hum was censored the minute she rocked the status quo and questioned the righteousness of keeping cradles vacant by abortion. Most folks, who were unfamiliar with pro-lifers, barely knew the wallflower existed.

Moreover, when an abortion protester was offered a seat at the table of newsworthiness, he or she was much more colorful than the wallflower. The only anti-abortion types that garnered media attention were usually mentally unstable and unattractively violent. Their despicable actions were totally out of step with the predominantly peaceful anti-abortion movement. Remember that hypocrite Clayton Lee Waagner?

This ultimate anti-abortion extremist was believed responsible for mailing white powder—fake anthrax—to 280 abortion clinics in October and November 2001. Waagner bathed in the mainstream media's mighty waters after Attorney General John Ashcroft declared him the subject of a national manhunt. He was also accused of threatening abortion clinic workers via e-mail earlier in 2001. Authorities captured Waagner in the parking lot of a Kinko's copy center outside Cincinnati later that year, before the fanatic could act upon his alleged threats.

The media often depends upon outrageous behavior of over-the-edgers to bring something new to old stories. And there's no denying that Waagner's capers made great copy.

In February 2001, while awaiting sentencing on firearms and car-theft charges, Waagner escaped from an Illinois prison. The jailbird then zigzagged across the country in fancy stolen cars, lived high on the hog for months, frequented bars, splurged on rounds of drinks, chain-smoked, and chewed the fat about the abortion issue. This outlaw allegedly supported himself by robbing banks. The father of nine, forty-five-years-old at the time, lodged in upscale hotels while his family, back in Kennerdell, Pennsylvania, remained in their one-story ramshackle house at the end of a gravel road.

This cancer on the image of the anti-abortion movement was sentenced to thirty years in prison on firearms, car-theft, and jail-break charges in January 2002. Waagner was also convicted of firearms possession and car theft in U.S. District Court during the spring of that year. In December 2003, a federal jury in Philadelphia found him—still unable to kick his criminal habits—guilty of making terroristic threats to abortion clinic employees.

Federal authorities say that Waagner will spend the rest of his life behind bars without parole due to his collective convictions.

Most anti-abortion activists abhor violence and feel equal aversion toward those who stoop to it in the name of life. When Waagner was apprehended, many right-to-lifers found themselves in agreement for the first time ever with Kate Michelman, NARAL's president at the time, who said, "I am immensely relieved that Clayton Waagner has finally been arrested."

People on both sides of the issue also heaved sighs of relief on the arrest and conviction of anti-abortion militant and murderer James Kopp. Kopp will serve twenty-five years to life for killing an obstetrician-gynecologist who performed abortions. The hypocrite who claimed to defend life took Barnett Slepian's life by firing an assault rifle into the doctor's kitchen window on October 23, 1998. The sniper who professed his concern for unborn babies left Slepian's four children fatherless when he deprived the doctor of life.

The publicity generated by anti-abortion wackos and kooks like Waagner and Kopp energized the media-savvy types who drive the pro-abortion movement.

For more than twenty years, NARAL has provided statistics to feed the media stories about people who used violence to oppose abortion. According to a list posted on NARAL's Web site, 7 murders, 17 attempted murders, 41 bombings, 122 assaults, and 165 arsons, among other crimes and attempted crimes, have been committed by extremists at abortion clinics since 1977. By weaving sensational stories about pro-life lunatics with statistics, NARAL yarn-spinners fabricated a pro-life stereotype.

Stereotyping, a power play, works in many different ways. For example, when I returned to Temple University in midlife to complete my bachelors' degree, I was immediately struck by my acquaintances' limited perceptions about the area around the university's main campus in North Philadelphia.

At first, friends delighted in hearing of my return to college in 1998. When fellow suburbanites asked, "What school?" and I replied "Temple," a few paused and others nodded weakly. Some simply stated their opinions. They acknowledged the school's fine reputation, and, then, asked me about my fear factor due to crime in and around Temple's urban campus.

Film footage of North Philadelphia, highlighted with yellow crime scene tape, regularly filled the first few minutes of local TV news. It still does. Reporters describe gunfire and sometimes murder, usually drug-related. Innocent adults and even children, along with criminals, are caught in the crossfire.

This TV view of one portion of the picture created hypertension about an entire section of a city and its residents. The sound-bite-fed-fear stereotyped an entire neighborhood. Since most of the people in North Philadelphia are of African descent, it also reinforced racial stereotypes for those inclined to be racist.

In reality, the hustle of bodies moving around Temple's main campus sharply contrasts media images of deadly activities in the area. Interspersed among the many members of the university's huge student body are neighborhood folks crossing the campus, children strolling to or from nearby schools and an occasional blank-eyed addict so battered by drug abuse that the only life in danger is the addict's own.

Other locals on campus include university employees working as security guards; parking lot attendants; and office, maintenance, and food-service personnel. More than a few of them log long hours during a workday at Temple. Some have children in college; others have children in jail. Just about everybody knows someone devoured by the dragon of the illegal drug trade, as people everywhere do. For that dragon breathes its hellfire in suburban and rural areas, too.

Since the many kind people I met on Temple's campus hardly

fit the media-induced stereotype, I decided to apply the same eyewitness approach to investigate the anti-abortion movement in my area to see if pro-lifers were truly as hypocritical as they appeared to be in news stories.

Just as I suspected, I tuned into a reality far different from media imagery. I found the immensely larger, peaceful portion of the right-to-life movement puttering along, sometimes prayerfully, without fanfare.

Pro-life fundraisers are not exactly digestible society page fodder. However, two annual banquets sponsored by Pennsylvanians for Human Life (PHL) offered those 500 or so of us in attendance each year plenty of food for thought.

John Haas, the affable president of the National Catholic Bioethics Center, addressed the heady topics of the ethics of genetic engineering, stem cell research, and abortion during the PHL 2001 gathering. Two years later, Donna Huttenlock talked about the abortion in her teens that led to self-destructive behavior and decades of depression, even during marriage and motherhood of two children years later. Her troubles stemmed from the loss of "her aborted daughter."

My appetite for answers about abortion also compelled me to join more than 1,500 people at the Pro-Life Union of Southeastern Pennsylvania's annual dinner in November 2003 to hear what their guest speaker, U. S. Representative Patrick Toomey, had to say.

The representative became unapologetically pro-life while preparing to challenge Senator Arlen Specter, a longtime supporter of abortion rights, for Specter's well-worn Senate seat in the 2004 Pennsylvania Republican primary. Yet, Toomey's past positions on the issue of abortion suggested he might be just another politician juggling with voters' emotions.

Toomey supported first trimester abortion rights during his

1998 campaign to represent Pennsylvania's Fifteenth Congressional District. The legislator also voted against "an amendment prohibiting the FDA from using any funds appropriated in this bill [HR 1906] for development, testing, or approval of any drug for the chemical inducement of abortion" in 1999.[1]

My irritation with Toomey's newly found affinity for pro-lifers ruffled me even more than earth-toned Al Gore's somersault from anti- to pro-abortion during the race for the presidency in 2000. During his cut-and-dried speech, Toomey dissipated my doubts and made me realize that there are still some politicians with deeply held convictions.

Improving American culture could only be accomplished with "willingness to speak the truth," Toomey said. The Harvard-educated—via scholarships, loans, and jobs—son of a union worker and a part-time secretary mother-of-six explained his change of heart about abortion.

The man who hoped to create a more fetus-friendly Senate stated that his past position on abortion and voting record on RU-486 "did not sit well" with him then. Around the same time, Toomey's wife became pregnant, and he saw their unborn little one on an ultrasound screen before the infant's birth.

Toomey admitted that his introduction to fatherhood brought him to the realization that "the life of the unborn baby is more important than the convenience of the mother."

The Senate seat seeker's words stopped me in my cynical tracks. For maternity had the same effect on me. Parenthood affected Toomey's politics (during the primary he lost by a narrow margin) in the same way that it altered my personal views about abortion. Fatherhood allowed at least one politician to hear the message of morality, which he had known all along in his heart.

Most of the people I found among the rattling knives, forks, and spoons at pro-life dinners never wrestled with such a change of heart about abortion. These folks possess such a simple and uncluttered sense of right and wrong that the culture could not turn their principles into Silly Putty.

Members of "the greatest generation," senior citizens who were veterans of the movement, were plentiful at pro-life banquets. Two retired obstetricians with plenty of prenatal and delivery room experience and expertise attended with their wives. A pair of unplanned grandparents, who had shaken off their initial shock upon learning of their single daughter's pregnancy and supported her throughout, now supported the pro-life movement whole-heartily.

As I moseyed, chitchatted, and eavesdropped among the women, men, and children of all ages at each pro-life event, I sensed sadness more than anger about abortion among those in attendance. Many lamented the missing children who will never be missed enough to warrant photographs on milk cartons or Amber Alerts.

The gentle demeanor of the folks at those pro-life banquets sharply contrasts that of the demented pro-life stereotype who hogged the news about anti-abortion activists for so long. Unfortunately, outlandish types supply the fodder that satisfies the public's hunger for sensationalism, which the media tosses to the public in bigger and bigger bales.

Times and tastes change, though. More fairness in coverage of the abortion issue appears to be creeping into stories about contradictory killers who claim to be pro-life. An *Associated Press* story by David Crary that ran in the *Philadelphia Inquirer* on September 1, 2003, makes my point.[2]

The gist of the story is that Paul Hill, a Presbyterian minister who gunned down a Florida abortion doctor in 1994, was to be "the first American executed for anti-abortion violence." The *Inquirer* labeled Hill's picture with the following caption: "Paul Hill, a minister, is not pursuing an appeal. He was disavowed by many anti-abortion activists."

In the article, abortion advocates voiced concerns that Hill would become a martyr for the cause and encourage copycat killers. Responses to those concerns came from people on both sides of the abortion issue in a neat display of Crary's balanced reporting. "'We need to take these threats seriously,' said Vicki Saporta, president of the National Abortion Federation," in one point of view. In another, "'We and other pro-life organizations are against violence, period,' said Erik Whittington of the American Life League. 'What he did was definitely not anything that anyone I know of supports.'"

This AP story about a murdering minister reads differently than many that contributed to the fabrication of a violent pro-life stereotype in bygone days.

Maybe more in the U.S. media are finally snapping out of the spell that abortion advocacy casts over them as facts unfold about the negative long-term effects of abortion. It has been legal for more than three decades now. Time is telling us that abortion has not magically led to all that glitters in the pot at the end of the gender-equality rainbow.

Chapter 9

Who, What, When, Where, Why Pro-Life

I f most pro-lifers are not lunatics for life, then who are they?
The camera was usually focused on a person wearing a
cross in the rare photographs of peaceful pro-life protesters
that have appeared in the mainstream media over the years.

Many anti-abortion groups are faith-based. There are Baptists for Life, Lutherans for Life, Presbyterians Pro-Life, and the National Organization of Episcopalians for Life. At least a dozen national organizations are identifiable as Catholic, including the ever-increasing presence of Priests for Life, in all areas of the pro-life movement.

Jews for Life was founded "to reflect the traditional Jewish pro-life perspective on abortion" in an online publication that addresses "the tragic consequences that have befallen women and our culture since *Roe v. Wade* was enacted into law."[1]

Brian Clowes lists ninety pro-life and pro-family organizations, including at least eighty major national and international prolife groups.[2] Still, a total count of individual pro-life activists in the United States is difficult to enumerate.

A simple Internet search turns up the names of other pro-life organizations that might surprise people, since pro-lifers have also been stereotyped as conservative or religious or both. There are Feminists for Life and Libertarians for Life, along with the Pro-Life Alliance of Gays and Lesbians. The Atheist and Agnostic Pro-Life League declares "a nontheistic and nonreligious opposition to the life-denying horror of abortion."[3]

I counted 157 registered members of the international Atheist and Agnostic Pro-Life League on the group's Web site in June 2003. Forty-two members favored complete abolition of abortion, 114 allowed for exceptions, especially when the life of the mother was threatened, and one member did not specify.

The Atheist and Agnostic Pro-Life League's membership numbers might not be overwhelming. But the existence of this group illustrates that one does not have to believe in the Bible or the words of David in Psalm 139:13, "For it was you [God] who formed my inward parts; / you knit me together in my mother's womb," in order to oppose abortion.

Yet, one hears little about these seemingly alternative pro-life groups in the mainstream media, especially if they are prone to be peaceful. One group of anti-abortion activists did garner some media attention in Pennsylvania last year because of their audacity.

The *Philadelphia Inquirer's* columnist John Grogan wrote about loudmouthed pro-lifers who were protesting outside of Planned Parenthood of Chester County. Members of the group carried graphic posters of late-term aborted fetuses and tongue-lashed women entering the clinic. Signs read: "Baby Killer." "You're murdering your children." "Slice and dice your baby." "You're sacrificing your baby to Satan."[4]

When I called Jo Christof, who heads the Chester County Pro-Life Coalition, to hear what she had to say about such obnoxinousness-in-the-name-of-life, she explained that "different people in the pro-life movement use different approaches to reach different audiences."[5] Christof protests outside of the same clinic on a different day with a different group that applies "a more toned-down approach with no yelling or hollering." Even though the impudent protesters' in-your-face method of trying to persuade pregnant women not to abort has never been Christof's style during her seventeen years of counseling against abortion, she was quick to point out that the screamers "have saved babies."

One mother returned to the Planned Parenthood clinic to show the boisterous anti-abortion activists her four-month-old baby. She told them that she had heard the demonstrators outside the clinic and was dissuaded from having an abortion. Reports of other women bearing babies, who returned to abortion clinics to express gratitude to the noisy protesters, have surfaced in both the Philadelphia and Harrisburg areas, too, according to the Chester County Pro-Life Coalition's president.

Turns out I was not the only one to contact Christof after reading the news about verbally badgering anti-abortion activists. The mother of two grown adopted children and grandmother of two was delighted to hear from an *Inquirer* editor who invited Christof to respond to Grogan's story that cast such a dark shadow on prolifers. Thanks to the fair-minded editor, Christof's *Commentary* essay was published within two weeks of Grogan's column in November 2003.[6]

Fortunately, some journalists do tip the scales in favor of balanced reporting by making room on their opinion pages for anti-abortion views. One *Philadelphia Daily News'* editor and three *Inquirer* editors made room for some of my anti-abortion essays in recent years (*Daily News* 4—*Inquirer* 3).[7] By publishing alternate views about abortion, views in contrast to their newspapers' consistent support of abortion rights in editorials, these editors abided by the Society of Professional Journalists' Code of Ethics:

Members of the Society of Professional Journalists believe that public enlightenment is the forerunner of justice and the foundation of democracy. The duty of the journalist is to further those ends by seeking truth and providing a fair and comprehensive account of events and issues.[8]

It's comforting to know that at least five editors in the birthplace of America's independence bucked the status quo and practiced the fairness that their profession preaches by publishing pro-life pieces.

I wish I could say the same thing about media coverage of the March for Life in Washington, D.C., on January 22, 2003, the thirtieth anniversary of *Roe v. Wade.* There were analyses of the issue and some news stories about women with emotional scars from abortion reported around the anniversary. However, newspaper and television accounts of the main event suggested a scene that did not reflect what I saw during my first political protest.

Today, many major news outlets tighten their conglomerate budgetary belts, skimp on reporters, and rely on news services for stories to fill space and airtime. It is possible that everybody referred to the same *Associated Press* account of the rally, which appeared in both of Philadelphia's leading daily newspapers, for information about the march.

The AP story began, "Opponents and supporters of abortion rights rallied at the nation's symbols of freedom yesterday, energized on both sides by Republican hopes of curbing the procedure thirty years after the Supreme Court legalized it."[9] Seems as if both those with thumbs up and those with thumbs down on abortion were out in full force on the anniversary of *Roe v. Wade* for "dueling protests."

This eyewitness begs to differ.

Because it was my first experience as a political protester, I studied my fellow dissidents with great attention to detail. As I squeezed into the Metro with masses of marchers for the underground ride into the heart of Washington, as I waited an hour on Constitution Avenue to exercise the First Amendment, and even as I chugged along weaving my way through miles of steambreathing people headed toward the U.S. Supreme Court building that frigid day I did not see one person bearing a banner in favor of abortion.

The crowd of anti-abortion activists was so massive that I never once rubbed elbows with the group of abortion advocates gathered near the Supreme Court building. Later, I learned that the official count for numbers of marching pro-lifers was estimated to be 200,000. This figure was nowhere to be found in the AP article, although one imbalance in numbers was noted in an exchange between "about twenty other pro-choice advocates" who "found themselves outnumbered by roughly fifty women carrying signs that read 'I regret my abortion.'"

The mainstream media had little more to say about those "roughly fifty women" who were members of the group Silent No More. Too bad! Group members might have filled newspapers and airwaves with some interesting stories if given the chance.

Georgette Forney, executive director of the National Organization of Episcopalians for Life, is one of the cofounders of Silent No More. She had an abortion at age sixteen, and knows the silence that follows: "We are the voice that hasn't been heard."[10]

And even the most quick-fingered remote-clicker learned little about the March for Life if he or she tuned into ABC or CBS or NBC news. The Media Research Center, a conservative watchdog group that eyeballs the media for bias, lambasted the major networks who "studiously ignored" the March for Life in 2003.

So what if it was the thirtieth anniversary of *Roe v. Wade*! So what if hundreds of thousands of near frost bitten pro-lifers marched! So what if Reuters estimated the count of pro-choicers who attended the midday Planned Parenthood rally to be a meager 150! CBS anchor Dan Rather told his viewers, "Tens of thousands of demonstrators on both sides of the issue filled the streets of Washington today."

The March for Lifers who "filled the streets" of D.C. and crossed my path that day were teens, tots, parents, spouses, singles, and grandparents. One free-spirited, gray-haired woman with a retro '70s look pushed her grandchild in a stroller while singing church hymns. A mischievous group of teens added mirth to the scene by marching along to the beat of their rhythmic chant, "your mother…(long pause)…chose life."

People bore bright banners and flags that identified their prolife groups and locations in the nation. Signs delivering the message "Women deserve better," that were distributed by the Feminists for Life of America, were plentiful in the crowd.

One man carried a homespun brown cardboard sign that packed an indelible markered message. It read, "1787—We the People. 1973—We the Supreme Court."

The Constitution of the United States was written in 1787. Its Preamble reads:

> We the People of the United States, in Order to form a more perfect Union, establish Justice, insure domestic Tranquility, provide for the common defence, promote the general Welfare, and secure the Blessings of Liberty to ourselves and our Posterity, do ordain and establish this Constitution for the United States of America.

The judiciary legalized abortion in 1973, not our legislators whom we elect to represent us. By legalizing abortion without absolute certainty about when life begins, as expressed in Section IX, Part

B of the Opinion of the Court, the Supreme Court justices showed no regard for "our Posterity."

Before noting that "the unborn have never been recognized in the law as persons in the whole sense," Justice Harry Blackmun wrote:

> Texas urges that, apart from the Fourteenth Amendment, life begins at conception and is present throughout pregnancy, and that, therefore, the state has a compelling interest in protecting that life from and after conception. We need not resolve the difficult question of when life begins. When those trained in the respective disciplines of medicine, philosophy, and theology are unable to arrive at any consensus, the judiciary, at this point in the development of man's knowledge, is not in a position to speculate as to the answer.

Where was the wisdom in making the fateful *Roe v. Wade* decision without proof of when life begins for "our Posterity"? Appointed Supreme Court justices, who ruled on *Roe*, bear a heavy ethical burden for legalizing abortion without answering "the difficult question of when life begins." "We the People" bear it with them.

Chapter 10

Is the Post-Roe v. Wade Generation Becoming the Conscience of Our Nation?

E ven though Supreme Court justices from the *Roe v. Wade* case admitted that they did not know when life begins, self-serving NARAL pushed its agenda with deceiving scientific language about the starting point of life. The media and, then, folks in general fell like dominoes for the group's hocus-pocus life-begins-at-birth conjecture.

Way back when NARAL was known as the National Association for the Repeal of Abortion Laws, it portrayed the unborn as clumps-of-cells. This description helped women to rationalize naming themselves as beneficiaries of the "Blessings of Liberty" promised in the Preamble to the U.S. Constitution with total disregard for their "posterity."

No wonder there were so many young people bopping, bouncing, and rapping to a life-begins-at-conception tune at the 2003 March for Life. More than a few old-timers told this newcomer to the yearly event that they had noticed annual increases in the numbers of high-school and college-age marchers since the late 1990s.

Others on the frontlines of the right-to-be-born movement have also noted an upsurge in counts of younger pro-lifers with post-*Roe* birth dates. A news item about this trend led me to an update by the Population Research Institute that offers plenty to ponder.[1]

Basically, pro-lifers have more children than those in favor of abortion and "like begets like," according to PRI's president Steven W. Mosher. Mosher credits Father Paul Marx, who has been teaching about life issues internationally since the 1970s, for bringing this to light.

Both Father Marx and Mosher noticed that "larger families than the average," some "with four, six, or even eight children," attended pro-life events. "It only made sense," they agreed, "that those who respect the sanctity of unborn life would average more children than those who do not."[2]

The two men turned to one of the top pro-life researchers, Human Life International's Brian Clowes, for statistics to back up their observations. Mosher reported Clowes conclusion, based on "sketchy survey data" available in the mid-1990s, that "pro-lifers averaged three children, while pro-aborts averaged one." This three-to-one margin led Mosher to conclude that "demography is destiny after all." With pro-lifers reproducing more than pro-aborts, "the ranks of the pro-lifers would swell while the ranks of the pro-aborts thinned. The pro-abortion movement would have signed its own death warrant."

Leave it to a journalist to come up with the perfect phrase, "the *Roe* effect," to describe what Father Marx and Mosher surmised and Clowes confirmed. James Taranto first used the term "The *Roe* Effect" in his "Best of the Web Today" column to describe his theory that the political effect of abortion is a more conservative America.³ "Best of the Web Today" is published in the *Opinion Journal*, which is an online publication of the *Wall Street Journal*. Interestingly, when Taranto dubbed it "The *Roe* Effect" on December 11, 2003, he was not responding to Mosher's article about pro-lifers producing more children which was published the day before. Instead, Taranto was commenting on another story that appeared in *The Christian Science Monitor* on December 10, 2003.

The *CSM* story by Amanda Paulson, entitled "Religious Upsurge Brings Culture Clash to College Campuses," details a notable rise in religion, especially evangelicalism, in the realm of higher education.⁴ This newfound fervor for faith on college campuses created tension between proponents of such spirituality and secularists.

Taranto quoted a couple of paragraphs from Paulson's *CSM* report before writing, "For just as the baby boom of the 1940s transformed campus culture in the 1960s, so the liberal baby bust following *Roe v. Wade* [the *Roe* effect] is producing a more conservative student body today."

Survivors of "the *Roe* effect" might also be more sensitive to the fragility of life because of their exposure to the blood and guts of violence in our society. Young Americans, the post-*Roe v. Wade* generation, have seen tragedies on our turf that babyboomers like me never imagined: newborns are found dead in dumpsters; children and teens are kidnapped, raped, and slaughtered; students shoot and sometimes kill students, teachers, and principals in school hallways; people of all ages with no connection to the dirty business of drug dealing die after being caught in dealers' crossfire; and terrorists crash airplanes into skyscrapers in order to murder masses on busy workdays. Our young people also know that they, too, could have been aborted.

One colorful pro-life youth group with a commanding pro-life march presence, Rock for Life, names its "enemy" as "the culture of death" and declares war in its literature. "You will not silence my message. You will not mock my God. And you will stop killing my generation."[5] The group's logo, complete with an illustration of a wailing-guitar-toting fetus in an amniotic sac, identifies the group as a division of the American Life League.

Rock for Lifers number more than 100 chapters across the country. They are "committed to offering the truth about abortion, infanticide, and euthanasia to America's youth through music and ministry."[6] These rockers also identify entertainers who support the "culture of death" and encourage fans to spend their disposable income on the works of those who are unabashedly pro-life.

Rock for Life appeals to a "broad audience" and serves as a good "alternative" to more conservative groups, Kim Marshall told me when we spoke in April 2003. Marshall serves as director of Generation Life, a youth group in the Philadelphia area that also participated in the March for Life of 2003. Generation Lifers regularly conduct prayer vigils outside of abortion clinics.

Generation Life "invites" young people to "build a culture of life" by beginning with chastity and saving sex for marriage, said Marshall. Speakers from the group visit elementary and high schools and present age-appropriate programs to deliver their message. Generation Lifers clarify how "sexual purity ties into pro-life" by noting the link between the Sexual Revolution, which kicked open the door to sex out of wedlock and the demand for abortion that followed.

Staggering statistics support Generation Life's position on the connection between no-marital-vows-sex and abortion, again courtesy of Brian Clowes in his book, *The Facts of Life, An Authoritative Guide to Life and Family Issues*. Unmarried women accounted for 1,215,350, or 80.1 percent, of the average annual number of 1,517,290 abortions from 1980 through 2000.

Moreover, 1,506,770, or 99.31 percent, of the annual number of 1,517,290 abortions from 1980 through 2000 were "lifestyle," or non-therapeutic abortions. (Therapeutic abortions include the "hard cases," abortions performed when the mother's life or health is at risk, when the pregnancy resulted from rape or incest and when testing predicts fetal birth defects.)[7]

In Marshall's experience, "students are hungry for the truth," and many young people approach discussions of sexuality with no-holdback "honesty." Students, who were sexually active but found that their lifestyle left them feeling unfulfilled, often take a pledge of chastity.

College students who surveyed their surroundings while passing the Bell Tower on Temple University's Main Campus in Philadelphia on October 14 and 15 in 2002 were probably not thinking about chastity. However, they could not help but think about abortion. For that's when Generation Life sponsored the Genocide Awareness Project at Temple.

The Genocide Awareness Project or GAP is a traveling mural exhibit. Some people consider GAP a radical approach to pro-life education. The Center for Bio-Ethical Reform (CBR), which works to "establish prenatal justice and the right to life for the unborn, the disabled, the infirm, the aged and all vulnerable peoples," developed GAP as one of its "cutting edge educational resources."[8]

A big orange sign displayed in an area near the GAP exhibit reads "Warning Genocide Photos Ahead." It is a warning best heeded if one tends to be squeamish viewing graphic photographs that depict historically just how low human beings can go.

There are pictures of Holocaust victims' corpses with sunken eyes in shaved heads and a blindfolded African American man hanging by his neck from a rope on a tree. Next to these shameful moments in European and American history are pictures of little bloodied aborted limbs and bodies.

Through comparison, GAP graphically depicts abortion as a contemporary abomination, a pox upon our nation. One mural aligns a trio of round photographs labeled "Extermination," "Lynching," and "Abortion," and asks the question, "Can you connect the dots?" By positioning flesh-and-blood photos of aborted fetuses next to those of people murdered because society labeled them "inhuman," The Center for Bio-Ethical Reform presents a strong argument that abortion is genocide.

The term *genocide* was first used to describe attempts by Adolph Hitler and his Nazi regime to exterminate the Jewish population during World War II. The CBR offers the following definition of genocide from a 1992 edition of *Webster's New World Encyclopedia.* Genocide is "the deliberate and systematic destruction of a national, racial, religious, political, cultural, ethnic, or other group defined by the exterminators as undesirable."

One GAP mural features a potential "undesirable" in thirty-eight colorful and incredibly beautiful images of the work-in-progress that is humanity within the uterus. If this zygote, then embryo, then fetus, is aborted sometime during that growth cycle, he or she will become like the ghastly pictures in the exhibit on genocide.

Perhaps the most disturbing GAP abortion photograph includes the familiar dime featuring the profile of President Franklin D. Roosevelt, a coin minted in 1946, one year after he died. The coin commemorated Roosevelt's ardent support of the March of Dimes. FDR was paralyzed from the waist down due to polio. Resting on the top of the shiny FDR dime in the GAP picture is a tiny dismembered arm with its hand touching the tail of the word *Liberty.* Delicate fingers on a detached hand lay on the bottom curve of the dime. There is blood in the background. This photo is labeled "First Trimester (10 weeks)."

GAP's graphic address to the ambivalent in a survival-of-the-most-self-centered society gives voice to the aborted. The limbs of this ten-week-old aborted fetus speak volumes even though the developing baby was permanently hushed by the misguided mentality that rationalizes the righteousness of abortion.

Perhaps this fetus was aborted because prenatal testing revealed some predisposition to a disease that would make him or her less than physically perfect like FDR? Perhaps not? Maybe he or she was destined for greatness like FDR? Maybe not?

That's the problem with abortion. We will never know.

Chapter 11

Legalized Abortion Is
Not Jane Roe's Choice

Norma McCorvey never counted on notoriety in 1970 when she added her voice to the pro-abortion chorus over beer and a slice of pizza in a Texas restaurant. That's when and where the self-described, sometimes homeless, "hippie" agreed to become Jane Roe, as in *Roe v. Wade*.

With a ninth-grade education and few job skills back in those early days of women's lib, McCorvey's chances of becoming a cross-country public speaker were not much better than her chances of being liberated. And you better believe that standing behind a wooden podium with a cross on it would have been the last place that McCorvey might have imagined herself in midlife. But that is where I found the straight shooter with a knack for spiking her speech with humor one Sunday in April 2003.[1]

McCorvey remembers that as a poor and pregnant twenty-two-year-old, all she wanted besides alcohol and marijuana back in her Jane Roe days was an abortion. It was McCorvey's third pregnancy, the second out of wedlock. A marriage she entered at age sixteen was already history. When two lawyers, described by

McCorvey as "ambitious," approached her about becoming the plaintiff in a case to overturn the Texas statute outlawing abortion, it sounded like a pretty good idea at the time. Hence, McCorvey, AKA Jane Roe, signed an affidavit for attorneys Sarah Weddington and Linda Coffee in March 1970. Nine months pass by quickly and cases often move slowly through the courts. The plaintiff never had the abortion. Instead, Jane Roe gave her "eight-pound baby girl" up for adoption, just as she did in her earlier pregnancies.

Since McCorvey never appeared at court hearings, she thought she had heard the last of her legalese identity until one January night in 1973. Jane Roe read and reread a newspaper account of the Supreme Court's ruling that legalized abortion in all fifty states, reached for a bottle of her favorite liquid painkiller, and drowned her dumbfoundedness.

McCorvey went on to employment in four Texas abortion clinics, continued to souse it up, and grew suicidal. She began to deal directly with patients while working for her third abortion-providing employer. But it was not until she was on the payroll of the clinic known as A Choice for Women that her behavior on the job became peculiar.

A combination of occurrences inside and outside the clinic affected McCorvey.

Since the recovery area was "bland, all white with red, and you know what the red was," McCorvey decided to decorate it with sunflowers. One morning, while outside collecting flowers, her good intentions suddenly turned into skies overcast with sadness when she burst into tears as she clipped blossoms from the bush.

While taking cigarette breaks outside of A Choice for Women, McCorvey grew more and more curious about the people next door who worked or volunteered at Operation Rescue, a national anti-abortion group that engages in peaceful protests and side-walk counseling outside of abortion clinics. The crew at Operation Rescue, who always seemed "so happy," fascinated McCorvey even though she considered them "sort of inhuman" at the time. McCorvey wondered why the group was so joyful going to work every day. When one woman from the group told the inquisitive one that the source of their joy was "Jesus," the seeds were planted for McCorvey's conversion to Christianity.

Meanwhile, McCorvey grew increasingly troubled by the apathetic way in which women were treated on entering A Choice for Women. When a woman mumbled or stated, "I am here for an abortion," she was typically "humiliated" with a curt, one-word response, said McCorvey. Jane Roe's work "in marketing" abortions did not blind her to the need for pre-abortion counseling. McCorvey decided to fill that need.

In order to be certain that these women knew what they were getting into, the unorthodox counselor developed a crash course that might best be described as show-and-tell. McCorvey not only explained the procedure, she showed patients the bloody speculums, the instruments used to dilate or open body passages for medical examinations.

On another occasion, McCorvey had a marathon phone conversation with a distraught mother who called the clinic to seek an abortion for her sixteen-year-old daughter. McCorvey had recently learned that her own daughter, with whom she had reconnected, was pregnant at the time. The mental image of an aborted grandchild appalled Jane Roe. As a result, McCorvey persistently tried to convince the mother that in choosing abortion for her daughter she would lose a grandchild. The woman whose livelihood now depended upon the abortion industry referred the caller to Operation Rescue before letting her off the hook.

This first referral was unplanned, but offering Operation

Rescue's telephone number to people who called the abortion clinic became a regular practice for McCorvey. It was not just the eyeful of the little pieces of humanity that were stored in the clinic's freezer that rattled her into action. After a particularly disturbing incident with one of the clinic doctors, McCorvey made referrals to Operation Rescue her standard procedure.

One day a doctor asked McCorvey "to go into the parts room and put a baby back together" after an abortion. "The abortionist had to account for every part, or he had to go back in," she explained. McCorvey's "that's not my job" response failed to dissuade the doctor. He "pulled me into the back and demanded that I piece the child back together" to see if the abortion was complete.

McCorvey felt justified after being forced to work with discarded body parts in asking for a raise. When the doctor refused, McCorvey spent her final days as an abortion clinic employee deliberately keeping the doctor's appointment book blank and reading Stephen King's books, one after another, to kill the time. Determined to put the clinic out of business, she referred callers to Operation Rescue for counseling. When the clinic closed, the next chapter of McCorvey's life began, a life full of strange twists like the fiction she favors.

The story of McCorvey's life climaxed when she was baptized and became a Christian in 1995. Two years later, McCorvey founded the nondenominational Roe No More Ministry, now called Crossing Over Ministry, because she wanted to tell America the truth about Jane Roe.

McCorvey added another twist to the narrative of her life by becoming a Roman Catholic in 1998.

The irony of the "former Jane Roe's" turn toward Catholicism cannot be ignored in light of the 1960s NARAL campaign. One of the founders of NARAL, Dr. Bernard Nathanson, admitted in his article [or book?], "Confession of an Ex-Abortionist," that the underlying tactic of the NARAL campaign was to vilify the Catholic Church by creating the illusion that only the hierarchy—not the laity—of the Church oppose abortion.[2] Advocates "fed the media such lies as 'Polls prove time and again that most Catholics want abortion law reform.' And the media drum-fired all this into the American people," who came to believe that Catholics who opposed abortion were mind-controlled by Church hierarchy, while those who favored abortion were "enlightened and forward-looking." The Catholic Church was singled out repeatedly, while the fact that there were other pro-life voices, Christian, non-Christian, and atheist, was "constantly suppressed."

The Christian Catholic McCorvey is the dog that's come back to bite NARAL. If you have ever had the opportunity to hear her speak, you know that this tough-talking truth-seeker is an independent thinker who is nobody's lackey. Even McCorvey's position as "100 percent pro-life" came with considerable thought over time.

McCorvey admits, "At first I thought abortion was OK in the first trimester, but not anymore." Her pro-life pals had their opinions and she had hers. The "full humanity" of the contents of a pregnant woman's womb "hit her" one day after viewing a fetal development chart that raised her awareness of an embryo's beating heart.

A child raised other awarenesses for McCorvey. Emily invited "Miss Norma" to come with her to church so many times that McCorvey finally went simply to appease the little girl. Emily is the daughter of Ronda Mackey, an Operation Rescue volunteer who befriended McCorvey.

"I put another face on abortion while watching Emily play at a playground three days after my Baptism," McCorvey explains. As Emily frolicked, McCorvey was overwhelmed by sadness, sorrow that inspired her to write a poem. "I know of such places where children play. I know that I am the cause of them not being here today," she wrote in *Empty Playgrounds*.[3]

If McCorvey has her way, abortion will be illegal someday. Her plan to fill more swings and sliding boards is twofold. In addition to her Crossing Over Ministry, McCorvey is committed to the Texas Justice Foundation's "Operation Outcry."

As McCorvey spoke to her Visitation audience, the cadence of her speech radically shifted when she fired away information about Operation Outcry—a group representing women who experience self-degradation rather than liberation after abortion. There were 5,000 women involved in Operation Outcry, McCorvey pointed out. The Texas Justice Foundation had already collected 2,000 testimonies from women who suffered after abortion. More than 3,500 to 4,000 Friend of the Court briefs were already on file in April 2003.

The Texas Justice Foundation, which is a nonprofit public interest law firm, represents McCorvey and Sandra Cano.

Cano is the "Mary Doe" of the landmark but less widely known abortion case, *Doe v. Bolton*. The U.S. Supreme Court ruled that abortions could be performed during all nine months of pregnancy if a doctor deemed it necessary in *Doe v. Bolton*. This decision was also made on January 22, 1973, the same day that abortion was legalized during the first trimester and if the state permitted during the second trimester in *Roe*.

Under Rule 60 of the Federal Rules of Civil Procedure, former plaintiffs McCorvey and Cano, Roe and Doe, could attempt to reopen their cases in hopes of having them overturned. "On motion and upon such terms as are just, the court may relieve a party or a party's legal representative from a final judgment, order, or proceeding," states Rule 60.

"The issue is justice for women, justice for the unborn, and justice for what is right," McCorvey said with conviction. So, she filed a "motion for relief for judgment" in order to reopen *Roe v. Wade* in June 2003.

McCorvey's motion was based on changed conditions and law. There are medical facts about abortion and its aftereffects that we know now, but did not know in 1973. Also, state laws in effect today allow states to care for unwanted children.

A federal district court dismissed McCorvey's request on June 19, 2003, two days after it was filed. "It is simply too late now, thirty years after the fact, for McCorvey to revisit that judgment," Judge David Godbey wrote in his ruling.

When McCorvey's attorney Allan Parker said his client would probably ask the court to reconsider its ruling, it came as no surprise. The legalization of abortion in the United States is a very personal matter for the "former Jane Roe." And this survivor of the sixties and seventies, with the slow and easy Texas drawl, has a lot of fight left in her.

Why does the founder of Roe No More Ministry keep fighting to end abortion? Because, she says:

> ...*Roe v. Wade*...
> is a case...
> not...
> based...on...truth.

Chapter 12

Moral Regression Impeccably Dressed As Progress

Moral regression impeccably dressed as progress is nothing new in the United States. Neither is splitting the truth at the seams to promote such pretense.

Americans of yesteryears dehumanized people of African descent and enslaved them in the name of progress. All that free labor not only lined the coffers of slaveholders, it boosted the economy. The first slaves were shipped like cargo into the United States in 1565. The Thirteenth Amendment abolished slavery in 1865. That's 300 years worth of tinkering with the truth to advance and preserve a pretense of progress.

This same systematic distortion of truth in order to advance the well being of some people at the expense of others has been polluting our environment for more than thirty-one years now. Today, the aborted pay the price with their birthright. Women who buy the delusion that abortion is necessary in order to advance gender equality seem willing to trade-off morals as a means to an end. Mothers who choose abortion lose a piece of their posterity in the deal.

Abortion advocates have long used a tactic that has been

effective in selling abortion as a must-have for women's rights. They apply a we-know-what-is-best-for-you approach toward other women when it comes to abortion. Ironically, this condescending modus operandi of feminists for abortion, who claim to know what is best for the rest of us, reeks of paternalism. And, isn't paternalism a practice that feminists find loathsome?

Paternalism is supposed to be a male thing. It involves an unequal distribution of power. *Pater* means "father" in Latin. Under paternalism, the party with the power maintains a relationship with underlings much like that of a father with his children.

The institution of slavery was effectively advanced and preserved by paternalism. Time has proven that the self-serving practitioners of paternalism who promoted slavery did not know what was best for slaves or society. One day, sooner or later, the truth will surface. Time is now proving that the self-serving practitioners of paternalism who promote abortion do not, in fact, know what is best for women or their offspring.

The paternalistic approach of abortion advocates toward maternity (*mater* meaning "mother" in Latin) failed to take into account the power of the maternal bonds, severed so unnaturally by abortion. This laceration of the lifeline from a mother to her unborn child leads to post-abortion trauma for more than a few women who choose abortion (see chapter 5).

Moreover, just as overworked or worked-to-death slaves suffered physically at the hands of those who claimed to know what was best, aborted children suffer before dying at the hands of abortionists and proponents of the brutal practice. Fetuses in the womb feel pain as early as the first trimester according to medical experts.

Pro-life advocates rely on the expertise of Dr. Vincent J. Collins, professor of anesthesiology and author of the textbook *Principles of Anesthesiology: General and Regional Anesthesia*, for truth about fetal pain. In Collins' opinion, "fetal pain responses begin by thirteen and one-half weeks gestation *at the latest*, and probably as early as eight weeks, based upon the development of the pre-born baby's nervous system."[1] The Center for Bio-Ethical Reform's Executive Director Gregg Cunningham is more medically specific in describing Collins' findings: "The neurological structures necessary to feel pain, pain receptive nerve cells, neural pathways, and the thalamus of the brain, begin to form eight weeks after fertilization and become functional during the thirteenth week."[2]

Despite the testimony of these experts, Planned Parenthood Federation of America (PPFA), our nation's leading abortion provider, maintains that "almost all abortions are performed before the capacity to feel pain develops."[3] The PPFA's online "Facts Sheet" reports that "55 percent of legal abortions occur within the first eight weeks of gestation, and 88 percent are performed within the first twelve weeks." Now, remember what professor of anesthesiology Collins said about fetal pain occurring somewhere between eight and thirteen weeks of gestation. "Fifty-five percent of legal abortions" is not "almost all." More accurately, that number is slightly more than half. Even if the embryos aborted in the 55 percent of abortions performed before eight weeks do not feel pain, it is possible that the remaining 45 percent of fetuses aborted, or fetuses in almost half of all legal abortions, do indeed feel pain.

And since the capacity to feel pain registers sometime between eight and thirteen weeks in gestation, some number of embryos or fetuses included in the 88 percent of abortions performed within the first twelve weeks must surely suffer. Therefore, suffering seems likely since embryos and fetuses are either sucked out of the uterus by a machine or sliced apart and removed from their mothers' wombs piece by piece during first trimester abortions.

Planned Parenthood attempts to push its pro-abortion agenda by shushing outcries over fetal pain with gibberish. PPFA's response to the question "Can an embryo or fetus feel pain?" is a lie by omission of an affirmative answer with specifics about fetal pain.

Mothers faced with unplanned pregnancies are vulnerable, and the difficult decision to abort must be made quickly. Denying women all of the facts about abortion does them a great disservice. As more veterans of abortion are realizing, abortion's permanent cessation of pregnancy leaves many of them feeling as if they have lost a part of themselves.

Once again, Planned Parenthood exhibits hollowness where there should be heart. If during the abortion procedure just one fetus feels pain, how can PPFA keep pretending that abortion is humane? The institution of slavery was supported by a similar mind-set.

This born-and-bred Northerner met that mind-set while sightseeing in Charleston, South Carolina. It was in the head of a genteel, well-groomed white southern lady who conducted a tour of one of the city's historic mansions for my husband Michael and me.

Our tour guide detailed the history of the magnificent Joseph Manigault House, a three-story Federal-style brick home with charming two-story porches that was built between 1803 and 1807. The Manigault family, we learned, descended from Huguenot ancestors who fled France near the end of the seventeenth century in order to escape religious persecution. As we toured the house and grounds, the guide described in detail the antebellum lifestyle of the Manigaults, a typical wealthy Charleston family: a lifestyle revealed in the mansion's many elegant rooms, each reserved for a particular function that catered to the family's every need; a lifestyle reflected in their privileged way of life, visible in the art work, furniture, and fine imported china; a lifestyle, as the guide pointed out, that included the luxury of "servants" who performed the various household functions.

Toward the end of our visit, Michael questioned our hostess. "The servants you've mentioned a number of times," he said, "they were slaves, weren't they?"

"Well, yes they were," she mumbled with downcast eyes.

Then, the well-spoken lady rattled off a story about a friendship between one of the Manigaults and a male slave. This particular family member and his slave had known each other since childhood. When the slave left the Manigault household after slavery was abolished, his master said, "I just lost my best friend." Yet, if a list of Manigault's assets were available, the value of his "best friend" would have been measured in the same monetary terms that determined the worth of the slaveholder's paintings, furniture, fine imported china and other assorted pieces of property.

With nonverbalization of the word *slave* amidst the splendor of that Southern mansion and the telling of a little vignette, perhaps our guide thought that the gritty realities of the institution of slavery would escape our memories. Abortion advocates hope we will develop a similar amnesia about the inhumanity of abortion when they define the procedure as "choice" and developing babies as potential liabilities.

The next stately historic home we visited in Charleston served as a metaphor for the right way to present a harsh reality. The Aiken-Rhett House, built in 1818, includes remnants of all of its former inhabitants' lifestyles. The original outbuildings behind the mansion include slaves' quarters, the stables, the coach house, privies, the cattle shed, and the kitchen where the slaves cooked food in the southern heat before they lugged it up the back steps leading into the main house and through the back door.

After my husband and I paid the price of admission, the pleasant gentlemen behind the desk passed a pair of headsets to us for an audio tour of the antiquated and somewhat beat-up, not-quite-restored Aiken-Rhett House. And I began to wonder if this walk through another era was worth the entrance fee. I soon realized that it would be an experience I will never forget. For the sounds and voices on the tape transported me back to the antebellum South and into the home of Governor and Mrs. William Aiken, Jr.

The entrance hallway of the Aiken-Rhett House was a masterpiece of white marble and black cast-iron craftsmanship. Throughout the mansion, huge chandeliers hung from high ceilings, life-size portraits decorated walls, and fine sculpture filled otherwise empty rooms. The glory of the mansion was evident; only, everything about the house was dusty, a subtle reminder of the grime that accompanied the glamour of the era, dirt that was once mandatorily removed by slaves.

Behind the master's house and across from the coach house, stood the slave quarters, occupying the upper floor of the stables. The space allotted to slaves for living quarters was not much bigger than the space that housed the family's coaches and buggies.

Eeriness accompanied us up the creaky narrow wooden steps, through the tight hallway, and into the tiny rooms that the slaves called home. Uneasiness permeated every corner of the slave quarters. It superseded more pleasant imaginings of congenial family life, a salve to the wounds of injustice for many a slave, that might have existed there.

Abortion is, as slavery was, legal. Yet, no matter how much advocates dress it up in legalese or adorn it in the language of the double-tongued, abortion discriminates just like slavery and its ugly stepsister racism. While a hangman's rope silenced some slaves and their descendants, a looped knife or curette slices the vocal cords of helpless fetuses during dilation and curettage abortions and denies them a birthright.

We are heavy on noble aspirations here in the United States.

Our indifference during centuries of slavery illustrates the sham we made of our high standards in the past. The hideous facts about chattel life in the land of the free did not appear in standard history textbooks until the latter part of the twentieth century. Even as awareness of those truths elevates our shame for past practices, we replace one injustice with another.

Developing babies are dismembered, decapitated, or poisoned, and scalded during abortions. Abortion advocates claim these aberrant acts of moral regression are advances in healthcare for women. Feminists for abortion can dress it up, but the cold-blooded cessation of motherhood through abortion cannot take women anywhere but down.

Chapter 13

Survival of the Selected

F risbees glided, footballs spun, and soccer balls sailed under blue skies over the fields below the Washington Monument in our nation's capitol one Sunday in 2003. Sunglassed sightseers strolled from the monument toward museums and memorials. Bicyclists peddled, runners ran. Just another springtime day in a democracy.

When the opportunity to visit Washington, D.C., for a weekend came my way, I started packing. I needed a break from research and writing about abortion. Our U.S. armed forces were putting their lives on the line then, as they navigated the Persian Gulf, aviated the air over Iraq, and crossed borders into the secret-laden society of the dictator Saddam Hussein; a visit to war memorials seemed appropriate.

While I strolled by the Lincoln Memorial, the Korean War Memorial, the Vietnam Veterans Memorial, and the planned site for the World War II Memorial, I thought about the self-sacrifices made by U. S. military personnel.

One afternoon I toured the United States Holocaust Memorial Museum. I hoped that a look into Adolph Hitler's legacy as a murderous thief of human rights might help me to ascertain just how low a freedom robber like Hussein might go. Dirty secrets about life in Iraq under that dictator continued to surface during the spring of 2003. U.S. soldiers were uncovering evidence of terror, torture, and death suffered by selected Iraqis under the vile regime of Saddam and his masochistic sons.

Despite my best efforts to take the weekend off from the issue of abortion, bits of Hitler's history reminded me that undesirables are removed every day in our democracy.

Hitler and his Nazi party committed their atrocities in the name of racial purity from 1933 through 1945. German women were rewarded for bearing lots of children, as long as those children were deemed "pure Aryan," to serve the state. Meanwhile, Jewish women and others on the Nazi's hit list were subject to diabolically induced indignities. Joan Ringelheim, director of oral history at the Holocaust Museum, asserts:

> Jewish women carried the extra burdens of sexual victimization, pregnancy, childbirth, rape, abortion, the killing of newborns, and often the separation from children. Jewish women's lives were endangered as Jewish women, as mothers, and as caretakers of children.[1]

More than 1 million infants and children deemed undesirable died in the Holocaust. Children were the first to be terminated by gas at the Auschwitz concentration camp, along with pregnant women and women with children. Other undesirable girls and boys were killed in one of four "Operation T4" euthanasia centers. These murdered children's remains became abused corpses when their cadavers were deemed desirable for genetic research aimed at disease control. God, rest their souls.

An average of more than 1.5 million developing children deemed undesirable in the United States have been aborted each year from 1980 through 2000. More than 44 million American girls and boys are missing due to abortion since its legalization in 1973. The remains of these aborted embryos and aborted fetuses' bodies become tiny abused corpses when their cadavers are deemed desirable for genetic research aimed at improving methods of birth and disease control. God, rest their souls.

Most of the 6 million people who were murdered under Hitler's "Final Solution" were Jews. Others were Roma Gypsies, disabled people, Catholic priests in Poland, homosexuals, Jehovah's Witnesses, Soviet prisoners of war, and political dissidents.

Hitler and his Nazis violated women and rationalized the demise of innocent people by claiming that they were defective in meeting the regime's standards of Aryanism. People with abnormalities were murdered or subject to forced sterilization in order to maintain those standards. The Nazis aborted the non-Aryan Jewish unborn or murdered non-Aryan Jewish newborns to ensure a "pure Aryan" population.

U.S. standards determining who comes with a warranty that guarantees entrance into this life have been stretched like a rubber band ready to snap since the U.S. Supreme Court ruled in *Roe*. When in uteri fetal testing predicts abnormalities or deformities, undesirable unborn infants are aborted in order to avoid possible baby imperfection. And, abortion advocates have long stressed the importance of the practice to end pregnancies due to rape or incest, which for some victims becomes a double whammy (see chapter 5). Advocates also stress the need for abortion to save mothers' lives when pregnancy threatens women's physical or mental health, which is an area wide open to interpretation and implementation of abortion by women and their doctors.

These purported needs for abortion are exaggerated. In fact, inconvenient pregnancies account for the vast majority of abortions in America. A few more statistics, again courtesy of Brian Clowes in his book *The Facts of Life, An Authoritative Guide to Life and Family Issues,* reveal truths about abortion that should give us goose bumps.[2]

Almost all, 1,506,770, or 99.31 percent, of the average annual number of 1,517,290 abortions performed each year in the United States from 1980 through 2000 were "non-therapeutic" or "lifestyle" abortions. The "hard-cases" that ended in abortion accounted for the remaining 0.69 percent.

These "hard-cases" included: 5,460 pregnancies (0.36 percent) terminated because of health threats to the lives of mothers; 1,420 abortions (0.09 percent) performed on victims of rape or incest; and 3,640 pregnancies ending in abortion (0.24 percent) due to in uteri testing that predicted birth-defective babies.

The scope of the injustices suffered by Hitler's victims did not smack the world in the face until concentration camps were finally liberated by Soviet, British, and U.S. troops in 1945. Upon touring the United States Holocaust Memorial Museum and entering the Permanent Exhibit, visitors are faced with a large black-and-white photograph that foreshadows feelings to come. The picture features groups of stunned American soldiers as they discover the horrors of the Ohrdruf concentration camp. The soldier's dazed expression repeats itself on the faces of the people touring the Holocaust Museum.

Most Americans, including women who have had abortions, would appear equally appalled if they were permitted uncensored tours of abortion clinics. For if sightseers peeked into back rooms or clinic freezers, they would find tiny parts of dismembered bodies and petite corpses with oversized heads, miniature versions of the human remains found in mass graves by soldiers entering concentration camps.

Many of the German people ignored the stench of Hitler's

crimes against humanity as they went about the day-to-day business of surviving under a dictator during World War II. Others, indoctrinated by der Fuhrer's propaganda, doused themselves in the stinking eau de cologne of complicity.

Those same scents of indifference and compliance pollute the United States today. We are so busy pursuing happiness that we have barely noticed the barbarism of abortion. Meanwhile, more than 44 million unborn children will never know a springtime day in a democracy because they were murdered and removed from their mothers' wombs.

History has much to teach us. When will we ever learn?

Chapter 14

The Smoldering

A dolph Hitler's collective acts of cruelty were not always named the "Holocaust." Then *News-Week* magazine first used the word to describe one of the mind-control methods applied by the dictator to manipulate the German people. When the Nazis torched mountains of censored books in raging bonfires, *News-Week* dubbed it a "Holocaust."

If Germany's outright censorship that supported slaughtering humans was a holocaust, then the contemporary U.S. mainstream media's pro-abortion bias and restraint in reporting more about a procedure that butchers the unborn is a "smoldering."

As my interest in the issue grew and I wanted to know more about abortion, I found little about it in the mainstream media during the mid-1980s and through most of the 1990s. I had already given up on women's magazines, which spouted plenty of advice on cooking up career enhancement or how to be a steamy sexpot. And, despite my homemaker status, recipes on how to make a nifty gelatin mold left me cold.

Since I prefer details in my news, I watch only a little television reporting. So I turned to my favorite medium for information, the black-and-white one that used to be read all over. I found most newspaper stories and editorials about abortion to be one-sided. News about pro-lifer-led violence at abortion clinics, along with appropriate outcries of hypocrisy, was often featured. Political stories informed readers about NARAL's latest endorsement of assorted candidates for various offices. And in almost every bit of abortion news, readers could count on a quote from the ever-enunciating Kate Michelman, NARAL's former president and best pal to pro-abortion politicians.

My instincts told me that there were truths deemed not fit for fairness in print smoldering below abortion stories that media powers chose to report. Violent extremists with pro-life pretense received such thorough coverage that reasonable people were led to the assumption that anti-abortion advocates were pointy-tailed creatures carrying pitchforks. The pro-lifers I knew at the time attended my church. And the only weapons these folks packed while protesting were rosaries for counting prayers as they prayed outside of abortion clinics.

Standard fare, too, were popular with the press NARAL-endorses-some-politician stories. The photographs or film that accompanied these stories were pretty much the same. Only the politicians' grinning faces changed.

Balanced reporting about the presidential race in 2000, however, granted at least one exception to the typical NARAL political endorsement story.

The news of Al Gore's steady opposition of abortion rights, below the news that NARAL endorsed him for president, raised journalists' radar about fishy motives of flip-flopper politicians. Nobody could accuse Gore of being ambivalent about abortion. While representing the people of Tennessee in the House and the Senate, he was against it. While seeking election to the presidency in 2000, newly earth-toned Gore was for it.

Michelman voiced NARAL's endorsement for then Vice President Gore in the midst of the presidential primaries: "In the face of serious threats to reproductive choice—in tough, tough fights, Al Gore stood strong time and time again to defend a woman's right to choose."[1]

The wannabe president's record suggested otherwise.

The National Right to Life Committee gave Gore an 84 percent rating for legislative voting that supported the anti-abortion movement's position from 1977 to 1984, years during his tenure in the U.S. House of Representatives. Gore's opponent for the Democratic candidacy in the presidential race, former New Jersey Senator Bill Bradley, admitted, "I'm very surprised that NARAL would endorse someone who had an 84 percent Right to Life record, when I have 99 percent NARAL record."[2]

Bradley questioned Gore's record on abortion during a January 2000 debate in New Hampshire and the vice president responded, "I've always supported *Roe v. Wade.* I have always supported a woman's right to choose." Yet, Gore repeatedly voted against public payment for poor women's abortions. He voted to include "unborn children from the moment of conception" in the definition of person in four civil rights laws in 1984.[3]

And as *Washington Post*'s columnist E. J. Dionne, Jr., wrote, Gore also described abortion as "arguably the taking of a human life" in letters to constituents in 1983 and 1987.[4]

With malice toward neither Michelman nor former Vice President Gore, their problems with long-term memory raise questions about their veracity—a polite word for truthfulness.

Michelman and NARAL have maintained considerable clout in affecting the actions of ambitious politicians over the years. But NARALites and their abortion providing chums—even those with big-buck interests in keeping the $400 million a year abortion industry legal—cannot control everything.

Medical science now helps in healing fetuses in uteri. Technology highlights the fetal mystique with pre-born babies' first pictures. And, lamentably, mothers lose pregnancies and sometimes their own lives in crimes committed by deranged predators. All of these occurrences nurture sound musings about the morality of abortion, even as Michelman's and her political pal's media soundbites become more saturated in spin.

While I continued to purchase newspapers, I could not buy lopsided journalism. It was a relief to read Bernard Goldberg's gutsy book, *Bias, A CBS Insider Exposes How the Media Distort the News*.[5] Finally, a respected journalist confirmed my suspicions. Even broadcast news was overweight with reporting that focused on one side of an issue and out-of-shape due to slim chances of hearing from the other side.

The Emmy Award winning journalist states, and I agree, that media bias "is not some sinister plot, but about how mostly liberal journalists tend to frame stories from a mostly liberal point of view."[6] The problem of bias in network news divisions has little to do with political partisanship:

> It's about how they frame the big issues of the day—feminism, abortion, race, affirmative action, even taxes. On these issues they are reliably and predictively left of center.[7]

Goldberg notes that viewers who are turned off by opinion-laced-and-based news are stating so with their remote controls and moving from network to cable news in search of reporting that respects the public's right to form its own opinion.

A find for many viewers has been FOX News' *The O'Reilly Factor*, TV's top-rated cable news program since 2000. Newsman Bill O'Reilly consistently clarifies the difference between reporting the news, news analysis, and opining during *The Factor*.

O'Reilly passes along FOX Chairman and CEO Roger Ailes'

favorite example of how a "big issue like abortion" is framed on ABC, NBC, CBS, and CNN news:

> They exclude voices in America like crazy. You don't see an articulate spokesman who's pro-life on the network evening newscasts. They'd rather show someone who just shot up an abortion clinic.[8]

When Goldberg asked O'Reilly to foretell the futures of network anchors Dan Rather, Tom Brokaw, and Peter Jennings, the journalist replied, "It's like the last days of Pompeii. They're desperately trying to hold on. They see the smoke."[9]

The same magazine that published the term "Holocaust" in conjunction with its coverage of Nazi book burnings stoked the fires below the smoldering of abortion-related news and created more smoke last summer. In 2003, the *Newsweek* cover photograph (June 9) featured a nine-week-old fetus in utero looking a lot like a baby in a bubble. The headline that accompanied the photo read, "Should a Fetus Have Rights? How Science Is Changing the Debate."

Science and technology have taught us much about occurrences inside an occupied womb since abortion's legalization in 1973. Remarkable photographs of embryos and fetuses swimming in uteri are drowning out arguments that life begins at birth. And as writer Claudia Kalb noted in *Newsweek,* "the very same tools—amniocentesis and ultrasound—that have made it possible to diagnose deformities early enough to terminate a pregnancy are now helping doctors in their quest to save lives" through in uteri fetal surgery.[10]

Two photographs accompanying Kalb's story illuminated the fetal mystique and fueled pro-lifers' fires. In one picture the tiny hand of a twenty-one-week-old fetus emerges from an incision in his mother's uterus and grips the tip of a rubber-gloved surgeon's finger during fetal surgery to correct problems associated with spina bifida. The hand has grown in the photograph on the opposite page. It rests by the side of khaki overalls worn by three-year-old, Samuel Armas. The boy with a sort of sweet shyness in his smile stands on a lush green lawn, where "Samuel likes bug hunting at home in Georgia."[11]

The image of Samuel's power-to-the-fetus fist popping out of his mother's uterus appeared in countless pro-life publications and can still be found on lots of anti-abortion Web sites. *Newsweek's* Kalb reported that the Armases have no problem with the pro-life movement's adoption of the amazing picture. "We're very glad it's gotten visibility," said Samuel's father Alex. "That wasn't our fetus, that was Samuel."[12]

Three years later, another cherished fetus achieved fame because a murderer did not treat him or his mother with the same dignity. Photographs of this fetus fill coroner's files in Modesta County, California.

Two corpses rose from the cold waters of the Pacific Ocean the week before Easter in 2003. First, the body of an eight-month-old male fetus still wearing the umbilical cord that had been his lifeline was found along the coast in the rocky San Francisco Bay area. The next day the trunk of his mother's body surfaced.

Laci Peterson disappeared on Christmas Eve of 2002. The first-time mother-to-be with the incandescent smile had already named her soon-to-be-born son Conner. A jury found Scott Peterson, Laci's husband and Conner's father, guilty of first-degree murder for killing his wife and second-degree murder for killing his unborn son after a five-month-long trial in 2004.

The push to recognize a pregnant woman's fetus as a victim in crimes that fall under federal jurisdiction was initiated after the discovery of Laci and Conner Peterson's bodies. On-air media types, who generally shun stories about dead fetuses, drew tons of attention to pending legislation by yakking endlessly about the tragedy.

The legislation was entitled the Unborn Victims of Violence Act. The bill sought to make it a separate crime to harm or kill a pregnant woman's fetus during federal crimes of violence, in crimes committed that violated the Uniform Code of Military Justice or when those crimes were committed on federal lands such as military bases and Indian reservations. Republican Representative Melissa Hart (Pennsylvania) authored the bill.

Lawmakers renamed the act "Laci and Conner's Law," even though their murders were not federal crimes, after Laci Peterson's mother wrote a letter to key Republican and Democratic legislators. In her correspondence, Sharon Rocha stressed the importance of recognizing two victims in crimes like the one that robbed her of family. "When a criminal attacks a woman who carries a child, he claims two victims. I lost a daughter, but I also lost a grandson," wrote the mother who surely never imagined such sorrow.

Newsweek's Debra Rosenberg reported that NARAL's then president Kate Michelman "sighs deeply" and "accuses lawmakers of exploiting the tragic case" when she learns that the Unborn Victims of Violence Act was re-dubbed "Laci and Conner's Law." "It's so crass, so offensive," Rosenberg quotes Michelman as saying: "It's part of a larger strategy to establish the embryo with separate distinct rights equal to if not greater than the woman."[13] (It might be worth noting here that the perfectly formed fetus found along California's coastline was far past the embryo stage of development. An embryo becomes a fetus around eight weeks in utero.)

In NARAL's narrow mind-set the unborn have absolutely no rights. "But Michelman does not want to appear callous,"

Rosenberg writes; NARAL's then president called the reporter back "to stress how terminating a wanted pregnancy is 'an especially heinous crime that deserves enhanced penalties'" for harm done to pregnant women.[14]

Laci Peterson's mother opposed the adoption of a "single-victim" or mother-as-the-only-victim amendment to the Unborn Victims' bill. She believes that "Congress would be saying that Conner and other innocent unborn victims like him are not really victims—indeed, that they never really existed at all. But our grandson did live. He had a name, he was loved, and his life was violently taken from him before he ever saw the sun."

People who reacted to "Laci and Conner's Law" as a threat to abortion rights and opposed it on those grounds were missing the point. According to Conner's grandmother:

> The Unborn Victims of Violence Act explicitly says that it does not apply to abortion, or to any acts of the mother herself. Having said that, I have no difficulty understanding that any legislator or group opposed to abortion logically would also support this bill to protect the lives of unborn children like Conner from violent criminal actions, and I welcome their support….What I find difficult to understand is why groups and legislators who champion the pro-choice cause are blind to the fact that these two-victim crimes are the ultimate violation of choice.[15]

"Laci and Conner's Law," which the U.S. House passed as the Unborn Victims of Violence Act in 1999, and again in 2001 passed in the U.S. Senate by one single vote; and President George W. Bush signed it into law on April 1, 2004.

Another story about fetuses, fascinating but lacking the sensationalism that merits major media fixation, suggests that developing babies who die within their murdered mothers are not the only unborn victimized by violence. In "Fetal Psychology," Janet Hopson writes of "a startling new picture of intelligent life in the womb" that Johns Hopkins University psychologist Janet DiPietro and other researchers "armed with highly sensitive and sophisticated monitoring gear" have discovered.[16]

Upon reading about "Fetal Alertness," "Fetal Movement," "Fetal Taste," "Fetal Hearing," "Fetal Vision," "Fetal Learning," and "Fetal Personality" in the story, one cannot help but wonder about the impact of abortion upon a fetus:

- By nine weeks, a developing fetus can hiccup and react to loud noises. By the end of the second trimester, the fetus can hear.
- Just as adults do, the fetus experiences the rapid eye movement (REM) sleep of dreams.
- The fetus savors the mother's meals, first picking up the food tastes of a culture in the womb.
- Among other mental feats, the fetus can distinguish between the voice of Mom and that of a stranger, and respond to a familiar story that is read.
- Even a premature baby is aware, feels responds, and adapts to the environment.
- Just because the fetus is responsive to certain stimuli doesn't mean that it should be the target of efforts to enhance development. Sensory stimulation of the fetus can in fact lead to bizarre patterns of adaptation later on.

Not only that, Hopson notes, "At thirty-two weeks of gestation—two months before a baby is considered fully prepared for the world or 'at term'—a fetus is behaving almost exactly as a newborn."

Left in the safe and nurturing environment of the mother's womb, the baby will continue to develop until birth.

With these findings about fetal lifestyle in mind, fetal destruction in the name of anyone's rights seems cruel and barbaric. Technology is telling us more about the fetus than anyone on either side of the abortion issue ever knew. Science inches closer to proof that women's rights most vocal faction's disregard for the fetal mystique is a fatal mistake of monstrous proportions. Yet, abortion advocates and many mainstream media outlets remain mum or avoid references to this aspect of the abortion issue.

Sparks are flying from the smoldering that has suppressed balanced and unbiased reporting about abortion in the mainstream media. Flames will continue to rise until we stop telling ourselves that one injustice can be extinguished by perpetuating another.

Chapter 15

Cousins in Crime

S ome crimes bear a striking family resemblance to abortion. Feticide is the intentional killing of a fetus in an illegal abortion. It is criminal. However, when an embryo or fetus is legally aborted in the United States, we hail that abortion as an exercise in equality, the mother as liberated, and the destruction of her posterity as a government-given right. Meanwhile, if a mother chooses to kill her newborn at birth or within hours of delivery, we lament the loss of innocent extrauterine life, question the mother's mental state, and label the act neonaticide.

When a baby is murdered during his or her first year of life, the killer commits infanticide. And, since Laci and Conner's Law was passed, the person who takes the life of a pregnant woman is considered both a baby killer and mother murderer and the crime a double "homicide," if it is a crime committed under federal jurisdiction.

No wonder people are confused about abortion.

A rickety fence separates legal abortion from illegal acts like feticide, neonaticide, infanticide, and homicide in the United States. The distorted mind-set that rationalizes such acts is not too far removed from the ideology that supports abortion rights.

After all, some degree of worthlessness must be attributed to humanity in order to support the idea that it is morally acceptable to treat developing Homo sapiens like weeds to be yanked from their mothers' wombs and raked away into oblivion.

Are the rationalizations below the rhetoric of abortion advocacy sending subliminal messages that support coldhearted and sometimes bizarre behavior toward fetuses, infants, babies, and even pregnant women in our supposedly civilized society?

While desired fetuses float and flip in their amnion sacs, castoffs have been found among the sludge in municipal wastewater treatment plants across the nation. Flushed or dumped fetuses surfaced in Des Moines, Iowa; Tulsa, Oklahoma; Fort Lauderdale, Florida; Yonkers, New York; Colorado Springs, Colorado; Philadelphia, Pennsylvania; and Tucson, Arizona, during the last decade.

Much mystery surrounds discoveries of dead fetuses among stinking sewage from toilets and sinks or gutters on our streets. Were they miscarried, stillborn, or aborted? Are their remains the waste left in the wake of illegal or legal abortions? Only their mothers or possible abortionists know for sure.

"There's no way of knowing" how a fetus winds up in a municipality's wastewater, a woman who has been in the wastewater business for twenty-seven years explained to me. Helen Rhudy is the supervisor of the Wastewater Management's Roger Road Treatment Plant in Pima County, Arizona, where two dead fetuses have been discovered over the years.[1]

"Contractors found the [second] fetus because they were sorting manually" since equipment at the plant was being updated, Rhudy told me. Old bar screens, like the one that caught the first dead fetus passing through the system, were being replaced with new enclosed models. "Because the fetus [in the most recent discovery] was not badly mangled, it had to come from close by; for turbulence in the system will tear whatever passes through apart."

Gail Hackney, an advanced outreach coordinator for the U.S. Environmental Protection Agency's 104(g) program, offered more specifics about "turbulence" in wastewater systems. (Hackney trains wastewater employees and educates politicians who are making decisions about spending on wastewater equipment.) The waste that passes through our plumbing into sewers and on to wastewater treatment plants is repeatedly pumped before it hits the grinder that is "like a giant garbage disposal. Byproducts of humans are usually ground up by that grinder," Hackney said. "But a few bodies make it through and end up on the bar screen, like the fetuses' and the homeless man [found in 1998]."[2]

Any woman who has suffered the loss of a baby through miscarriage (before the twentieth week of pregnancy) or stillbirth (after the twentieth week of pregnancy but before delivery) understands how her embryo or fetus might have wound up in wastewater. I will spare you, my reader, and women like me who know such loss the unpleasant details.

Kathy Sparks' testimony about her brief career in one Illinois abortion clinic suggests that legally aborted fetuses could also be turning up in wastewater. Sparks, the executive director of the New Beginnings Pregnancy Centers in Fairview Heights, Glen Carbon, and Granite City, Illinois, is now unapologetically pro-life. Her three and one-half months as a medical assistant in an abortion clinic back in 1978 led to a change of mind about abortion. A spiritual conversion changed her heart.[3]

Sparks makes it clear that not all abortion clinics operate the same way. She believes that profit drove the assembly-line-like operation where she learned the ropes. Ninety-nine out of one hundred women agreed to abort after receiving counseling there.

While working in the cleanup room at the abortion center,

Sparks jarred and labeled embryos and fetuses of "twelve—thir- teen weeks or less" like preserves in preparation for shipment to the pathology lab. This particular clinic was not equipped for abortions beyond the first trimester, but that did not stop the operators from performing them and destroying the evidence:

> Oftentimes, second trimester abortions were performed and these babies we would not put in the little jar with the label to send off to the pathology lab. We would put them down a flushing toilet. They had a toilet that was mounted to the wall, and it was a continually flushing toilet; it didn't have a lid or a handle. That's where we would put these babies. They knew that they couldn't turn them in or they were going to be found out that they were doing abor- tions, which were too late term. This is what I participated in while I worked there.[4]

Could it be that operators of other abortion clinics are making aborted fetuses disappear the same way? Given the cloak-and- dagger nature of the operation, it is difficult to say.

No shiny blue balloons danced in the breeze to declare "It's a boy!" for one who might-have-been-a-newborn in 1994. His six- or seven-month-old fetal self was found at Iowa's Des Moines Waste Water Treatment Plant in August of that year. Strangers granted the fetal cadaver dignity after death. Iowans for Life pro- vided a funeral and buried the unknown fetus in the city's Glen- dale Cemetery, according to the *Des Moines Register*.[5]

When an employee at Tulsa's wastewater treatment plant found a fetus in a sewage disposal unit in June 2002, he prepared a grave nearby and buried the tiny corpse. Later, the worker re- ported the incident to a supervisor who called authorities in Oklahoma to investigate, revealed *U.S. Water News Online*.[6]

The remains of "a human fetus" found in the filtration system of Florida's George T. Lohmeyer Regional Wastewater Treatment Plant in October 2002, as reported in *The Miami Herald*, "would be impossible to trace" because the plant collects wastewater from several other communities in addition to Fort Lauderdale."[7]

A twelve-inch female fetus, "apparently stillborn," with her umbilical cord still attached was discovered during the cleaning of a machine at the North Yonkers Pump Plant in January 2003. She was not the first fetus found at that New York wastewater treatment facility. Two years earlier, Infinity Radio's 1010 WINS reported that an employee found an aborted male fetus in the equipment.[8]

Denver's *ABC 7 News* reported that the mother of a fetus, discovered at the Colorado Springs wastewater treatment plant in March 2003, would probably never be identified. An autopsy revealed that the less than 20-week-old Colorado fetus, found among solid waste that was being loaded onto a dump truck, was "apparently the result of a miscarriage."[9]

A water department employee in Pennsylvania spotted a fetus with the umbilical cord still attached in the sludge within an intake area of Philadelphia's Northeast Water Pollution Control Plant in June 2003. The *Philadelphia Inquirer* reported that the fetus was male and appeared to be white. Homicide detectives ended their investigation into the cause of the fetus' demise after the Philadelphia Medical Examiner's Office determined that the "3-pound" fetus, "estimated to be in the sixth month of development," was "stillborn," according to the weekly *Northeast Times* newspaper.[10]

Bob Purvis of Tucson's *Arizona Daily Star* reported that workers found a six-inch fetus "while scraping debris off a grate used to catch material like rags and sticks" at Wastewater Management's

Roger Road Treatment Plant in September 2003. Purvis quoted company spokesperson Laura Hagan Fairbanks who said, "You could see it and know it was human" of the fetus determined to be under twenty weeks of age.[11]

While fetuses are being flushed or dumped, newborns are being abandoned.

If landscape worker Rodrigo Sandoval Nunez had simply disposed of the sealed trash bag that he found hidden among evergreens outside of a bank on Philadelphia's busy Broad Street in the summer of 2002, tiny Tamara Doe would have died. Instead Nunez ripped open the black sack that moved to the beat of an infant's wailing and found a blood-covered newborn.

An eyewitness described the bundle as a "little girl with a full head of black hair, bluish eyes and a nice pink complexion." A police spokesman declared the infant just five minutes away from death. Nunez referred to his discovery of Tamara as a "milagro, or a miracle," according to the *Philadelphia Daily News.*[12]

Baby Tamara, named by the nurses at Children's Hospital of Philadelphia, faced near doom at birth by being placed in a plastic death trap. Even so, this infant could have been discarded and legally dumped if her mother had chosen abortion when Tamara was her former embryonic or fetal self.

Are desperate mothers like Tamara, mothers who are often isolated in some way or in deep denial about their pregnancies, rationalizing the perverse notion that newborns can be trashed like legally aborted embryos or fetuses?

The killing of offspring is nothing new. This practice, which seems so primitive, has occurred throughout the ages and in most cultures. "Neonaticide is not widespread, although we are more aware today as the twentieth century ends of instances of child-killing," wrote Lita Linzer Schwartz and Natalie K. Isser in their book, *Endangered Children: Neonaticide, Infanticide, and Filicide.*[13]

The authors noted a drop in crimes of neonaticide "as family planning spread at the end of the [nineteenth] century and abortion became more common....Neonaticide declined as convictions for abortions rose precipitously."[14] Poverty, as opposed to the shame that drove women in Victorian Europe to abandon babies, was the driving force behind the killing of newborns in the United States during the nineteenth century.

Even though we have had contraceptives aplenty for ages in America, and even though abortion has been legal for thirty-one years and the unmerciful stigma that once mortified unwed mothers has gone the way of girdles, women are still abandoning their offspring. Comparative U.S. Department for Health & Human Services' Administration for Children and Families statistics for 1991 and 1998 reveal a surge in baby abandonment.

This increase in the numbers of abandoned babies occurred during years when the economy, as members of President Bill Clinton's administration (1992–2000) regularly reminded us, was robust. On the other hand, some might argue that when the federal government rid itself of the Aid to Families with Dependent Children welfare program in 1996, it also encouraged despondent mothers lacking support systems and other aspects of life's necessities to do the same with their new babies.

Picture this. If all of the babies who were deserted in hospitals in 1991 and 1998 were gathered together, they would fill all of the seats in The University of Pennsylvania's Franklin Field—the oldest two-tiered stadium in the United States. In 1991 there were 21,600 babies abandoned in hospitals. There were 30,800 babies abandoned in hospitals in 1998. That's an increase of 43 percent in seven years.

Sixty-five babies were abandoned in public places in 1991. In 1998 the number increased by 62 percent when 105 babies were left to fend for themselves in public places. Many did not fare as well as the "little girl with a full head of black hair, bluish eyes and a nice pink complexion" in Philadelphia. Eight of the 65 infants abandoned in 1991 died and 33 of the 105 infants dumped after birth in 1998 met the same sad fate.

Who are these babies and their mothers who abandon them? A few more DHHS statistics reveal one thing many have in common. More than half of the babies abandoned in hospitals were drug exposed. The count came to 79 percent in 1991 and 65 percent in 1998. Sexual discrimination was not an issue in newborn abandonment. Almost equal numbers of infant boys and girls were abandoned in both 1991 and 1998.

While African American babies accounted for 75 percent of those abandoned in 1991, that number dropped to 56 percent in 1998. Meanwhile, the number of white babies abandoned in 1998 nearly doubled when it rose from 12 percent in 1991 up to 21 percent in 1998. The same pattern followed for abandoned babies of Hispanic descent, whose numbers jumped from 8 percent to 14 percent. A rise was also seen in the number of babies of "Other" races from 6 percent in 1991 up to 10 percent in 1998.

This trend we wish would end just will not go away. Even after 45 states introduced "safe haven" laws, laws that allow mothers to abandon newborns at hospitals and other assigned places with no questions asked, too many babies are still being abandoned illegally. More than 100 newborns under the age of 3 days were abandoned in the United States in 2000 and 47 of those infants died. These morbid endings of maternal responsibility solve nothing. In most cases, "mothers who have abandoned and/or murder their newborn children suffer from a lifetime of anguish and despair over choices made in a moment of desperation."[15]

Other moments of desperation result in murders of pregnant

women and their unborn children, like Laci and Conner Peterson. Unfortunately, that grim case is not the exception to the rule. Recent studies indicate that the leading cause of death among pregnant women is homicide.

Researchers from the Maryland Department of Health and Mental Hygiene combed through Maryland's death certificates, live birth and fetal death records, and medical examiner records that were dated from 1993 through 1998. Isabelle L. Horon and Diana Cheng hoped to determine causes of "pregnancy-associated" deaths in order to find ways to prevent such deaths. The results of their study were published in the March 21, 2001, issue of *The Journal of the American Medical Association*.[16]

Horon and Cheng focused on 247 "pregnancy-associated" deaths of Maryland women between the ages of fourteen to forty-four. The women died while pregnant or within the first year after delivery. Twenty percent of the group, 50 of the 247 women, died as a result of homicide. The second leading cause of their deaths was "cardiovascular disorders," which killed 48 women, or 19 percent, of the group.

Horon and Cheng concluded: "This enhanced pregnancy surveillance led to the disturbing finding that a pregnant or recently pregnant woman is more likely to be a victim of homicide than to die of any other cause."

Concerns about underreporting of "maternal mortality," led Cara J. Krulewitch to examine 651 autopsy charts from the District of Columbia's Office of the Chief Medical Examiner.[17] Women ages 15 to 50, who died from 1988 through 1996, were included in the study. Among the 651 cases reviewed, the records of 30 women indicated evidence of pregnancy. Of these 30 pregnant women who died, 13 women, or 43 percent, died due to homicide.

During the same period, the District of Columbia's State

Center for Health Statistics reported only 21 pregnancy-related deaths, all due to medical complications. The 13 pregnant murder victims, whose stories were buried in the paperwork and discovered by Krulewitch, were not included in the state's statistics of pregnancy-related deaths, and, therefore, were also not included in national counts. Krulewitch concluded that the more we know about homicide as a killer of pregnant women, the more we can do to prevent it.

So what do murders of pregnant women have to do with the issue of abortion?

If news within the news is any indication, maybe more than meets the eye. The murders of two pregnant women, who were killed in the 1990s, are directly linked to their decisions about abortion. Both of the deceased refused to have abortions despite pressure from their self-centered significant others, who fathered the children, to abort.

Joseph Peck claimed he gave a diamond-and-emerald tennis bracelet to his wife, Jennifer, just before her disappearance in 1995. Maybe he did. There is no doubt that the piece of jewelry was a gift to the criminal justice system when it turned up seven years later inside a duffel bag that belonged to Joseph. The satchel had Jennifer's blood on it.

Jennifer's body was found in the trunk of a car parked outside of a strip club in Tampa within days of her disappearance in 1995. She was twenty-four years old and four months pregnant at the time of her death. Her killer's weapon of choice was a claw hammer. Joseph was arrested and charged with his wife's murder in 2002.

According to coverage of the case by the *Associated Press,* "prosecutors said Peck killed his wife because he was unhappy about her pregnancy. They say she refused to have an abortion. Court records also state that Jennifer Peck told a counselor her husband was abusing her."[18] A jury deemed these allegations credible. Joseph Peck was found guilty of first-degree murder in a Hillsborough County Circuit Court and faces life imprisonment.

A former wide receiver for the Carolina Panthers is also serving time for a similar crime. Rae Carruth and four other men were arrested and charged with first-degree murder after one of Carruth's girlfriends, Cherica Adams who was pregnant with his child, was shot while driving her car in 1999.[19]

Cherica slipped into a coma and died within a month of being bullet-ridden. Chancellor Lee Adams, the baby boy she carried, survived the shooting after an emergency Cesarean section. Carruth was convicted of conspiracy to commit murder.

Carruth was dealing with injuries, money issues, and a nearly expired Panthers' contract during Cherica's pregnancy. The athlete already paid child support for a son in California and had invested badly in both financial schemes and friendships with thugs. While Carruth juggled his problems, Cherica prepared to be a mother.

Apparently Carruth had other ideas about becoming a father for the second time.

Both Cherica Adams and Jennifer Peck refused to submit to the will of the poor-excuses-for-men in their lives. These women died because they could not be coerced into having abortions. Their deaths are two too many. If I were a betting woman, I would put my money on the hunch that other pregnant women in abusive relationships have died for their convictions not to abort. Too bad such hunches are so tough to prove.

Remember how difficult it was for researchers to unveil the fact that predators end the lives of the pregnant. Details of those deaths were hidden below statistics of what we would rather think—health problems, not homicides, kill pregnant women. We would also rather think that when a woman has an abortion, she makes the choice. That notion is neatly tucked away in the envelope of secrecy that hides the details of abortion.

As women increasingly unseal their lips about past abortions, anecdotal evidence suggests that plenty of men choose abortion for the women in their lives. What's more, when some pregnant women choose birth, their deeply disturbed partners perform a distortion of abortion. These self-centered men rid themselves of responsibilities they do not want by permanently ridding themselves of the women who carry their children.

Simply put, homicide kills unwanted pregnant women and their posterity. Infanticide kills unwanted babies. Neonaticide kills unwanted newborns. Feticide kills unwanted fetuses. Abortion ends unwanted pregnancies.

Wait a minute. Abortion does more than end unwanted pregnancies.

Whether abortion is legal or illegal, it is basically the same procedure albeit under different standards of sanitization and quality of care. Like feticide, legalized abortion kills unwanted fetuses. Why abortion and feticide could pass for twins! And abortion, neonaticide, and infanticide could be close cousins. Too close.

Chapter 16

Motherspeak About the Fetal Mystique

A s publication of this book seemed remotely possible, I had one thing to do before typing "The End." I needed to call upon a dear friend. I had to tell her about the topic of my manuscript. I had to explain to her why I wrote it. I had to let her know what I learned about the aftereffects of abortion. I dread our meeting.

My friend had had an abortion. It saddened me so when she told me her secret years ago. Although I often wondered how that abortion had affected someone so sensitive, I never asked. I did not know how. Even though we scratched below the surface of everyday life and discussed the riddles of human nature during our many gab sessions, I feared that my questions about her abortion would be intrusive.

I arranged to see her and forced myself to tell her that my book about abortion would soon be published. Our get-together was much like the weather that day: partly cloudy, occasional showers, and some sunshine. And after I babbled my reasons for calling on my friend, it rained pain.

She let him talk her into the abortion. She did not know why. She never told her mother about her pregnancy or the abortion. Her now-deceased mom never had the chance to know her grandchild. Her baby would have been this and that by now.

In my friend's words, I heard the voice of Jeanne Stagloff, the lionhearted woman who allowed me to write about her post-abortive problems. And I remembered what psychotherapist Theresa Burke wrote in her book—*Forbidden Grief: The Unspoken Pain of Abortion*, about the aftereffects of post-abortive guilt and regret. Thanks to these women who shed light on the dark sides of abortion, I finally had some rays of hope to offer to my friend.

My apology for bringing along the cloud that burst during our visit was dismissed with a hug and a whispered "thank you." Not only that, our conversation about abortion continues. My friend suspects that a gentle soul dear to her might also be in need of post-abortive support and will offer that young woman a shoulder as needed. Finally.

Chances are we all know someone who is suffering in solitary after an abortion, since more than 44 million legal abortions have been performed in the United States since 1973. Because of the hush that hovers around a mother-to-be's abortion, countless women move freely among us who are still secretly chained to their post-abortive pain.

In fact, half of the women who choose abortion make the same choice at least one more time. According to Karen Patota, founder of A Baby's Breath, a Pennsylvania crisis pregnancy center,

This problem of repeat abortions is not due to callousness or the careless use of birth control. Instead, it is far more likely that women who have multiple abortions are "careless" in their birth control practices precisely because they are caught in a pattern of reenacting their traumatic abortions.[1]

If a single incident of such trauma in a woman's life leaves emotional scars for a lifetime, the emotional as well as physical damage from multiple abortions is understandably greater. When abortions after unplanned pregnancies tore someone dear to Karen Patota apart, Patota wished that the woman whose identity she closely guards had some place other than Planned Parenthood available to her for sorting out options. Instead, "Planned Parenthood told her they were removing a mass of cells from her," Patota recalls. Patota would not say how many previous abortions the woman had had, but noted that multiple abortions are common.

Patota's anguish over another woman's losses drove her to make the wish for an alternative to Planned Parenthood come true. A Baby's Breath, a crisis pregnancy center headquartered in Jeffersonville, Pennsylvania, opened on August 15, 2000. Since transportation or cash for bus fare to Jeffersonville were hard to come by for some clients, a second branch that is more accessible was created in nearby Norristown three years later.

Supported by a dedicated crew of helpers, Patota, forty-two, a homemaker, mother of four, homeschooler, and former engineer created A Baby's Breath "to help a mother to see her child take his/her first breath." She serves as the president of the all-volunteer "Catholic and Christian" faith-based group and director of the Jeffersonville center.

A Baby's Breath in Jeffersonville is housed in a grand old brick building with "West Norriton Consolidated School 1913" carved over the main doorway. It seems fitting. For the pregnancy counseling center is also a place of enlightenment.

Women faced with unplanned pregnancies enter A Baby's

Breath through a doorway discreetly tucked into one side of the old school building. They arrive alone, with partners, friends, or family members. The folks at the center welcome all parties interested in the mother-to-be and her pregnancy. Everyone is encouraged to take advantage of A Baby's Breath's referral and counseling services.

Some mothers-to-be who talk to counselors at A Baby's Breath are referred to other organizations, such as adoption or drug and alcohol addiction agencies, depending upon their needs. Women who have had abortions and suffer from post-abortive stress are invited to participate in a support group that meets once a month at the center.

Those counseled will find "absolutely NO graphic pictures of abortion here...ugh, I cannot even look at them," Patota told me when I visited the center.[2]

Sometimes women choose abortion and go elsewhere. One case made staffers "feel especially sad for the mother who lost an opportunity to know God in a very special way," wrote Patota in ABB's newsletter. "Every mother who has ever given life to a child and anyone who has looked into the face of an innocent baby knows God's love."

The mostly single mothers-to-be who decide to take advantage of services available to them at A Baby's Breath receive free pregnancy tests. They are assessed and evaluated for GED high school equivalency programs and are tutored at the center to help them complete their GEDs. In addition, they receive information about resources for housing or medical assistance, if needed. Mothers are also given the opportunity to attend classes or watch videos about parenting or childhood development and encouraged to meet with counselors or parenting support groups.

Participation in A Baby's Breath programs earns a mother credits to be totaled and exchanged for items she chooses from the group's Baby Store, a place that is a testament to the generosity of strangers who feed and clothe babies they will never know. Picture a room the size of an end zone, one filled with baby needs. Think bundles and giant plastic tubs full of diapers, shelves loaded with baby bottles and shampoo, food and formula (both always free to clients), and bibs, tables filled with comforters, receiving blankets, colorful crocheted afghans, a round rack stocked with baby clothes in every pastel imaginable, snowsuits hung neatly on another display, diaper bags and pails, rattles, teddy bears, books, toys, a stroller, and more. Large pieces of baby furniture are stored at another location, while maternity clothes for clients hang in an adjoining room.

The warmth of this fetus-friendly place overwhelmed me. Patota's alternative to Planned Parenthood, where mothers-to-be actually plan parenthood, soothed like a lullaby. Twenty to thirty volunteers hum along and keep it running. A Baby's Breath's leaders set the tone.

Besides the reverent ringleader Patota, I met two of her associates during my visit. One was a soft-spoken former preschool teacher, mother of four, and Director of the Norristown branch: Michele Pisano, thirty-two. Pisano wears her commitment to the women she serves with gentle enthusiasm, grace, and humility.

My second new acquaintance was the Baby Store's Donations Coordinator Kim Granito, thirty-eight, a former clinical researcher in the pharmaceutical industry and mother of two. Granito ran like a flash into the Baby Store. As she buzzed about checking on supplies for the center's clients, her inquisitive preschooler trailed her. The little guy fired away question after question. And his mother did not miss a beat in answering him.

Somewhere these women learned how to mother. By passing that priceless skill along, they have become like women of goodwill throughout the ages—feminists for others. You will not find their pictures in any of those stories about women worth admiring that are featured in the mainstream media. The inspirational subjects of most stories about successful women are usually powerhouses in business, the world of fashion, entertainment or the arts. Yet, what job is more important than being a good mother? And the rhythms of motherhood begin during pregnancy.

That tiredness so familiar to pregnant women foreshadows days to come when they will really be dragging after the baby arrives. Those lively nocturnal fetuses, the ones who kick and wake their dozing mothers, not only interrupt slumber but they set the stage for night feedings after birth. The nausea suffered by most mothers-to-be prepares them for that unsettling feeling a mother just cannot seem to shake whenever her child is sick. Let's not forget the rocking motion into which a woman automatically shifts when she balances a baby on her hip. Babies find this movement comforting because it mimics the swaying familiar to them when they were their former fetal selves.

U.S. Supreme Court justices demonstrated an absence of Solomon's wisdom when they recklessly tampered with the mysterious rhythms of maternity in their ruling on *Roe v. Wade*. Even legalese on the lips of the most learned cannot add cadence to blank spaces that once held the promise of more than 44 million beating hearts.

Abortion perverts the poetry that is procreation.

Epilogue

Deep down in our hearts, most of us know that abortion is morally wrong.

Truth cannot be completely squelched by self-deception. Sooner or later the truth about any injustice surfaces. Then our wrongdoings pretending to be rights shame us.

Blushing about abortion in America is becoming more common.

Time is telling. So are women who have chosen legal abortion in the past thirty-one years. Many mothers who aborted are breaking their vows of silence and revealing the dark side of abortion. They speak of painful aftereffects of a so-called solution that emptied them of motherhood and filled them with all sorts of self-destructive pollution.

Increasingly, former abortionists and abortion clinic workers are letting the rest of us in on the gruesome details of fetal destruction—crushed heads, tiny limbs torn from trunks, burnt little bodies—pieces of humanity that are as disposable as diapers.

Even science and technology have a thing or two to say that favors fetal rights these days. Put your focus on pictures of fetuses undergoing surgery in uteri. Take a peek into a preemie ward at your local hospital and see how fetal viability is being stretched even more by science. Find a pregnant family member or friend and accompany that mother to her next appointment for a sonogram. Look at her unborn human being on the ultrasound screen. Then, try telling yourself that abortion is humane.

Many folks whose instincts inform them that abortion is immoral are hesitant to declare themselves pro-life. These decent people have no desire to invade the privacy of someone considering abortion or hurt the feelings of anyone who has already had one. Nor do they wish to be associated in any way with the image they perceive to be pro-life. Advocates of abortion, with help from their friends in the media, have portrayed most pro-lifers as narrow-minded enemies of women, religious fanatics, or crazed killers. These pro-life stereotypes are inaccurate, as are all stereotypes.

In researching the anti-abortion movement, I came to realize that there is no mold that makes uniform pro-lifers. They come in blue jeans or khakis, adorn themselves with pearls or tattoos, wear dreadlocks or frosted hair, and bear rosaries or posters with graphic pictures of aborted babies. As it is with any group, the few who make the most noise receive maximum attention even though they do not represent the vast majority.

Writing this book also forced me to identify myself as pro-life. It was easier than I thought it would be, even when people disagreed with me. Nothing beats honesty.

Are you passively pro-life? If you are, please don't keep your ethics to yourself. Unborn lives are depending upon your values. Mothers faced with unplanned pregnancies might welcome your support. Women who aborted their unborn could use your compassion.

There are plenty of ways to be pro-life. Conversation about abortion over the kitchen table is a good start. Prayer is a powerful means of pleading your case. Serving as a volunteer at a pro-life organization or crisis pregnancy center helps babies and mothers, too. Peaceful protest is a more public way to express your point of view.

Mum should no longer be the word on abortion. It is time to break the barrier of silence surrounding the issue. The truth about abortion, like all truths, needs to be told.

Notes

Chapter 1

1. At least 44,670,812 abortions have been performed since legalization in 1973, according to the National Right to Life Committee. (The NRLC's abortion count is drawn from figures provided by both the Centers for Disease Control and the Alan Guttmacher Institute, Planned Parenthood of America's research affiliate that tracks the abortion industry.) National Right to Life Committee, "Abortion in the United States: Statistics and Trends," *National Right to Life,* http://www.nrlc.org/abortion/facts/abortionstats.html.

2. Serrin Foster, "Women Deserve Better" (lecture, Villanova University, Villanova, PA, February 23, 2003).

3. Bernard Nathanson, "Confession of an Ex-Abortionist," *About Abortion,* http://www.aboutabortions.com/. Dr. Nathanson writes extensively about his conversion to the pro-life cause in his autobiography, *In the Hand of God A Journey from Death to Life by the Abortion Doctor Who Changed His Mind* (Washington, D.C.: Regnery Publishing, 1997).

4. Brian W. Clowes, *The Facts of Life: An Authoritative Guide to Life and Family Issues* (Front Royal, VA: Human Life International, 200), 345–367.

Chapter 2

1. Babyland General Hospital, "History and Folklore," Original Appalachian Artworks, Inc.: Cabbage Patch Kids, http://www.cabbagepatchkids.com.

2. Stanley K. Henshaw, "Abortion Incidence and Services in the United States, 1995–1996," *Family Planning Perspectives* 30, no. 6 (November/December 1998), http://www.guttmacher.org/pubs/journals/3026398.html.

Chapter 3

1. David Crary, "Abortion Foes Hope to Sway Pregnant Women with Ultrasound Images," Associated Press State & Local Wire, February 1, 2001.

Chapter 5

1. Theresa Burke, "Post Abortion Syndrome" (lecture, St. Norbert Parish, Paoli, PA, April 13, 2003).
2. Ibid.
3. Ibid.
4. Theresa Conroy, "Tearful Victim Tells of Post-Rape Abortion," *Philadelphia Daily News*, January 16, 2004.
5. David C. Reardon, Julie Makimaa, and Amy Sobie , eds., *Victims and Victors* (Springfield, IL: Acorn Books, 2000), 15.
6. Ibid., 15.
7. Theresa Burke and David C. Reardon, *Forbidden Grief: The Unspoken Pain of Abortion* (Springfield, IL: Acorn Publishing, 2002), 114.

Chapter 6

1. Jeanne Stagloff, interview by Marybeth Hagan, May 29, 2003.
2. Margery Williams, *The Velveteen Rabbit Or How Toys Become Real* (New York: Double Day, 1922), 5.

Chapter 7

1. Betty Friedan, *The Feminine Mystique* (New York: W.W. Norton & Co., 1963).
2. Ibid., 72.
3. Feminists for Life of America, "Voices of Our Feminist Foremothers," http://www.feministsforlife.org/history/foremoth.htm.
4. David M. Kennedy, *Birth Control in America* (New Haven: Yale University Press, 1970), 113.
5. Clowes, 336.
6. Ibid.
7. Ibid.
8. Care Net, "Abortion in Black America: Statistics," http://www.abortionin blackamerica.com/.
9. Ibid.
10. Clowes, 337.
11. Ibid.
12. Ibid.
13. Ibid.

14. American Association of University Women, "Women at Work (2003)," http://www.aauw.org/research/womenatwork.cfm.

15. Ibid.

Chapter 8

1. Project Vote Smart, "Key Vote: Drugs Chemically Inducing Abortion," http://www.vote-smart.org/issue_keyvote_detail.php?vote_id= 2333&can_ id _ Cpa97913.

2. David Crary, "Abortion-clinic Killer Faces Execution, Amid Backlash Fears," *Philadelphia Inquirer*, September 1, 2003.

Chapter 9

1. Bonnie Chernin Rogoff, "As Pro-Life Jews: We Will Not Be Deceived by Choice," Jews for Life, http://www.jewsforlife.org.

2. Clowes, 345–367.

3. James Matthew Wallace, "Homepage," Atheist and Agnostic Pro-Life League, http:// www.godlessprolifers.org/home.html.

4. Jon Grogan, "Antiabortion Bullying for All," *Philadelphia Inquirer*, November 10, 2003.

5. Jo Christoff interview by Marybeth Hagan, November 18, 2003.

6. Jo Christoff, "Different Kind of People Unite Against Abortion Outside Clinic," *Philadelphia Inquirer* (Metro Commentary), November 24, 2003.

7. Marybeth T. Hagan, "Abortion Stereotypes & 'Code Words,'" *Philadelphia Daily News* (Daily Views Op/ed), February 1, 2002; "NARAL's Ultrasound Double-talk," *Philadelphia Daily News* (Daily Views Op/ed), February 28, 2002; "Why I'm Skipping the Rendell Primary Shuffle," *Philadelphia Daily News* (Daily Views Letters), April 16, 2002; "I Get Toomey's Change of Heart," *Philadelphia Daily News* (Daily Views Op/ed), December 9, 2003; "The Dark Shadow of Abortion Eclipses 'Twinkle' in One's Eye," *Philadelphia Inquirer* (Commentary), August 17, 2001; "Re-education of a Pro-Choicer," *Philadelphia Inquirer* (Commentary), January 22, 2004; "On the Beach, Advice on Sex and Safety," *Philadelphia Inquirer* (Metro Commentary and South Jersey Commentary), July 2, 2004.

8. Society of Professional Journalists, "Code of Ethics," http://www.spj.org /ethics_code.asp.

9. Associated Press, "Both Sides Mark Roe Anniversary," *Philadelphia Daily News*, January 23, 2003.

10. Karen Cross, "'Silent No More': Regret Over Abortion the Theme of Rallies Across the Nation," The National Right to Life Committee, February 2003, http://www.nrlc.org/news/2003/NRL02/karen.html.

Chapter 10

1. Susan Brinkman, "Winning the Cradle War," *The Catholic Standard and Times* (January 29, 2004).
2. Steven W. Mosher, "The Coming Demographic Victory," *Weekly Briefing,* December 10, 2003.
3. James Toranto, "Best of the Web Today," *Wall Street Journal: Opinion Journal,* December 11, 2003, http://www.opinionjournal.com/best/?id=110004415.
4. Amanda Paulson, "Religious Upsurge Brings Culture Clash to College Campuses," *Christian Science Monitor,* December 10, 2003.
5. Rock for Life, "Stop Killing My Generation" (Stafford, VA: American Life League, 1999).
6. Rock for Life, "Music buyers beware—What does your favorite band support?" (Stafford, VA: American Life League, 1999).
7. Clowes, 340.
8. The Center for Bio-Ethical Reform, "About Us," http://www.cbrinfo.org/about_us.html.

Chapter 11

1. Norma McCorvy was a guest speaker at Visitation Parish, Trooper, Pennsylvania, April 27, 2003.
2. Nathanson, "Confession of an Ex-Abortionist."
3. Norma McCorvy, *Empty Playgrounds,* Crossing Over Ministry (formerly Roe No More Ministry), http://www.roenomore.org/crossing_over/welcome.html.

Chapter 12

1. Clowes, 175.
2. Gregg Cunningham, "Abortion and the New Disability Cleansing," The Center for Bio-Ethical Reform: Resources, http://www.abortionno.org/Resources/natrev.html.
3. Planned Parenthood, "Abortion: Choosing Abortion Questions and Answers," Planned Parenthood Federation of America, Inc., http://www.plannedparenthood.org/ABORTION/chooseabort1.html (accessed May 21, 2003).

Chapter 13

1. Joan Ringelheim, "Preface to the Study of the Women and the Holocaust," Women and the Holocaust, http://www.womenandtheholocaust.com.
2. Clowes, 340.

Chapter 14

1. William J. Lutz, "Statement of NARAL President Kate Michelman: Endorsement of Al Gore for President," *Common Dreams Progressive Newswire News*, February 2000, http://www.commondreams.org/news2000/0215 -09.html.

2. CNN.COM, "Bush Unveils Campaign finance proposal; Bradley camp steams at Abortion Rights Group's Gore Endorsement," Cable News Network, February 15, 2000, http://cnn.com.

3. Richard L. Berke and Katharine Q. Seelye, "Now, Democrats Take a Turn at the Abortion Battle," *New York Times,* January 30, 2000.

4. E. J. Dionne, Jr., "Abortion: No Room for Ambivalence," *Washington Post,* February 1, 2000.

5. Bernard Goldberg, *Bias: A CBS Insider Exposes How the Media Distort the News* (Washington, D.C.: Regnery Publications, Inc., 2002).

6. Goldberg, 192.

7. Goldberg, 191.

8. Goldberg, 190.

9. Goldberg, 191.

10. Claudia Kalb and Mary Carmichael, "Treating the Tiniest Patients," *Newsweek,* June 9, 2003, 48–51.

11. Kalb, 49.

12. Kalb, 48.

13. Debra Rosenberg, "The War Over Fetal Rights," *Newsweek,* June 9, 2003, 44.

14. Rosenberg, 44.

15. Sharon Rocha, Letter sent by Sharon Rocha to key congressional sponsors of the "Unborn Victims of Violence Act," National Right to Life, http://www.nrlc.org/Unborn_Victims/sharonrochalettertokeysponsors.html.

16. Janet Hopson, "Fetal Psychology," *Psychology Today,* September/October 31, no.5 (1998), 44.

Chapter 15

1. Helen Rhudy, interview by Marybeth Hagan, March 5, 2004.

2. Gail Hackney, interview by Marybeth Hagan, February 2004.

3. Kathy Sparks, "Personal Testimonies: Former Abortion Providers Share Their Stories," Priests for Life, http://www.priestsforlife.org/testimony /sparks/html.

4. Ibid.

5. Tom Alex, "Male Fetus Found at Waste Water Treatment Plant," *Des Moines Register,* August 3, 1994.

6. *U.S. Water News Online,* "Archives: Plant employee finds fetus in waste-water treatment plant," *U.S. Water News,* June 2002, http://www.uswaternews .com/archives/arcsupply/2plaemp6.html.

7. Daniel de Vise, "Treasures, Trinkets Dot the Filth of Local Sewage Treatment Plant," *Miami Herald* (Broward edition), August 10, 2003.

8. 1010WINS.COM, "Fetus Found at Yonkers Treatment Plant," MMIII Infinity Broadcasting Corp., January 21, 2003, http://www.1010wins.com /topstories/local_story_021133848.html.

9. Denver's *ABC 7,* "Mother of Flushed Fetus May Never Be Found," Internet Broadcasting Systems, Inc., March 11, 2003, http://thedenverchannel.com.

10. Thomas J. Gibbons, Jr., "Workers Find Fetus in Sludge at City Waste-Treatment Plant," *Philadelphia Inquirer,* June 5, 2003; *Northeast Times,* "Fetus Found at Water Plant," June 12, 2003, http://www.northeasttimes.com /index.html.

11. Bob Purvis, "Fetus found at Sewage Plant," *Arizona Daily Star,* September 16, 2003.

12. Dan Geringer, "Newborn Found in Trash Bag by Landscaper," *Philadelphia Daily News,* August 27, 2002.

13. Lita Linzer Schwartz and Natalie K. Isser, *Endangered Children: Neonaticide, Infanticide, and Filicide* (Boca Raton, FL: CRC Press, 2000), 25.

14. Ibid., 31.

15. Laurie Krupp, "From the Director: What Are We Learning About Newborn Abandonment?" Safe Place for Newborns, http://www.safeplacefor newborns.com.

16. Isabelle L. Horon and Diana Cheng, "Enhanced Surveillance for Pregnancy-Associated Mortality—Maryland, 1993–1998," *Journal of the American Medical Association,* March 21, 2001.

17. Cara J. Krulewitch, "Hidden From View: Violent Deaths Among Pregnant Women in the District of Columbia, 1988–1996," *Journal of Midwifery & Women's Health* 46, no. 1 (January 2001).

18. Associated Press, "Tampa Jury Begins Hearing Case of Slain Pregnant Wife, *Naples Daily News,* September 4, 2003; "Tampa Jury Convicts Oklahoma Man in Pregnant Wife's Murder," *Naples Daily News,* September 11, 2003.

19. James C. McKinley, "Beneath the Smiles, A Tangled Relationship," *New York Times,* December 21, 1999.

Chapter 16

1. Burke and Reardon, 148.

2. Karen Patota, interview by Marybeth Hagan, October 8, 2003.

About the Author

Marybeth T. Hagan is a freelance writer whose work has appeared in numerous newspapers including: *The Christian Science Monitor, The Catholic Standard and Times, The Philadelphia Inquirer, The Philadelphia Daily News, The Delaware County Daily Times,* and *The National Catholic Register.*

The essayist recently completed her bachelor's degree in journalism at Temple University in Philadelphia. That college degree and wordsmithing are gifts that came later to her in life. She worked as a local bakery salesgirl, a telephone company service representative, a supermarket checkout clerk, a secretary on a college campus, in an advertising agency, a tabloid newspaper's offices and a tourism bureau, an NFL cheerleader for the Philadelphia Eagles, an aerobics instructor, and a department store makeup artist and salesperson over the years. All of these positions taught the writer much about the mysteries of human nature.

Ms. Hagan's most challenging and rewarding occupation is the one that lasts a lifetime—being a mother. She shares the ups and downs of parenting with her husband and partner of twenty-one years, Michael, a father who lavishes his love and the fruits of his labor on the family. Their home, a nest that is beginning to empty, is in Havertown, Pennsylvania. Firstborn Melanie attends Catholic University of America, while her siblings Amy and Mike whiz through high school.

The author wonders why she found her writer's voice, why she was one of the lucky ones born of caring parents, why she was given three good guys for brothers, why Michael Hagan walked into her life one crazy night, why she landed in a large family of loving in-laws, why she's been blessed with three healthy children and why miscarriages ended the promise of their sisters or brothers. She can only guess that it is God's will.